SUBVERSION:
Propaganda, Agitation and the Spread of People's War

Newspaper headlines every day give unavoidable prominence to the international activities of revolutionaries and terrorists. In this book Ian Greig traces the rapid development of the art and practice of People's War and its impact, examining both the historical background to subversive political movements, from the anarchists of the late nineteenth century onwards, and the major subversive forces now present throughout the world, including the Tupamaros, Black Panthers, Al Fatah, Viet Cong, Japanese Red Army, PLO, International Socialists, IRA and Black September.

The movements that have formed to change the 'system' derive their motives from any one of the socialist ideologies, from the desire for power in their own hands, or from sheer fanaticism. Their methods have been subtle or violent, and usually both. Ian Greig describes those who wage People's War, their aims, their means of support and training, and the channels by which the continuous process of revolt somewhere in the world is maintained and ensured by those whose own system was won, or is being won, by such methods. The horror of Munich has brought home to all of us that no country can ignore this reality.

SUBVERSION:
Propaganda, Agitation and the Spread of People's War

IAN GREIG

Tom Stacey

First published in 1973 by
Tom Stacey Ltd.
28-29 Maiden Lane, London WC2E 7JP

Copyright © Ian Greig 1973

ISBN 0 85468 450 6 hardback
ISBN 0 85468 495 6 paperback

Printed in Great Britain by
The Garden City Press Limited
Letchworth, Hertfordshire SG6 1JS

Contents

List of Illustrations

CHAPTER 1

A Look Backward

The story of revolt against authority, whether that of tribal chief, monarch, church, parliament, or dictatorship, is as old as history; but the evolution of sophisticated theories of revolution and subversion, their systematic application and the appearance of that increasingly familiar figure, the professional revolutionary, is a comparatively recent development.

Prior to the outbreak of the American and French Revolutions the great majority of revolts and revolutionary movements that studded the course of the centuries were essential aspects of power battles within the governing élite, involving the aspirations of rival claimants for the throne, the resistance of the noble or the increasingly important merchant classes to what they deemed the tyrannical or unjust edicts of monarchs, or fiery religious beliefs, rather than any great intention to change the lot of the common man for the better. In these circumstances the role of the 'revolutionary agent', whatever the cause, lay more in suborning the allegiance of members of ruling houses, the aristocracy, or government by outright gift of money, or promise of honours and advancement to come, than by any great effort to arouse mass support among the largely illiterate and apathetic people; who knew only too well that, whoever came out on top, they would probably remain at the bottom.

In the days when most landowners of any importance could rely on an unthinking personal loyalty or fear of eviction to quickly raise an imposing private army from the ranks of their tenants to support any cause of their choice, there was little need for widespread attempts at revolutionary organization or 'political education' amongst those whose allocated role was in any case little more than that of cannon-fodder. The battle was almost entirely for the minds of the influential.

One of the first mediums used by political propagandists eager to catch the eye of the lower strata of society was the political pamphlet, the production of which became a considerable vogue in Europe during the eighteenth century. The art of 'pamphleteering' became a popular one with many parties and factions; but with none more so than the British revolutionaries of those days: the Jacobites. During their prolonged struggle against the rule of the House of Hanover their agents on the continent and those working under cover in Britain itself poured forth a stream of highly inflammatory pamphlets; lampooning the reigning monarch and his Government and seeking to prepare the ground for revolt. A number of journals were also produced to add their weight to the attack which, taking the form of a sustained campaign, became a matter of serious concern to successive British governments.

One stratagem used by the authorities of the day to smash this campaign and the threat of armed Jacobite insurrection was that which has proved to be the bane of revolutionaries throughout the ages, infiltration of government agents into their ranks. One known to have been recruited for service against the Jacobites in this way was Daniel Defoe, author of *Robinson Crusoe* and himself a prolific pamphleteer. Recruited by Lord Townsend, Secretary of State, he reported in the spring of 1717 that he had succeeded in getting himself attached, on pretext of being a Jacobite sympathizer and in 'the disguise of a translator of foreign news', to a journal owned by a leading Jacobite sympathizer, Nathaniel Mist, who ran the paper as an organ for the Stuart Pretender. Defoe wrote:

> 'Upon the whole . . . by this management, the weekly journal [Mist's] and Dormer's letter, as also the *Mercuries Politicus*, which is in the same nature of management as the journal, will always be kept (mistakes excepted) to pass as Tory papers, and yet be disabled and enervated so as to do no mischief or give any offence to the Government.'[1]

[1] Richard Wilmer Rowan and Robert G. Deindorfer, *Secret Service*, William Kimber & Co. Ltd. (1969), p. 105

The then still comparatively new art of pamphleteering was to play an extremely important part in the events leading up to the French Revolution. For a host of pamphleteers were to put into popular and easily assimilable form the ideas and theories of Voltaire and other progressive writers; and so make them readily available to the more educated and frustrated members of the populace, who in turn passed them on to the illiterate masses. Here the pamphleteers were fulfilling a role vital to the accomplishment of any revolution dependent for its success on mass support: that of acting as a 'transmission-belt' which brings the ideas of the theoreticians to the notice of those whose support can be the means of putting theory into practice. And yet it would seem to have been more a contagious spreading of ideas, from which sprang new hopes and enthusiasms sweeping all before them like the waters from a bursting dam, that led to the swift spread of the revolutionary cockade all over France, rather than the existence of any detailed planning or sophisticated organization.

There were, however, two groups of revolutionaries active at this traumatic time which do have features of considerable interest as regards the practice of revolutionary techniques. The first of these was the group surrounding the renegade Duke of Orleans. At the height of the crisis, these ardent revolutionaries established a headquarters in the Palais Royal which quickly became a focal point for the direction of propaganda and agitation. Each night, thousands of revolutionary supporters streamed out of the city to assemble at the Palace and receive new instructions, pick up new slogans, and also perhaps money. Even more importantly this group centred on the Palais Royal was instrumental in turning the troops of the Paris Garrison from their loyalty to King and Government.

This they accomplished by the production of a spate of tracts and pamphlets especially intended for distribution amongst these troops, who only two months before had been obediently firing on the mobs in the Paris streets. The results were soon apparent. Before long even soldiers from the ranks of the crack Garde Française were demonstrating and shouting, 'Long live the Third Estate', or, 'We are soldiers of the nation'.

The other group with importance for the subject of this study was the group which appeared at the tail end of the Revolution in 1796, and consisted of a number of extreme radicals grouped around François Noël Gacchus Babeuf, a fiery journalist of extreme views. The group was dedicated to bringing down the existing revolutionary Government and substituting for it one more in keeping with their own views on 'equality'. Within three months they formed a network of agents covering the whole of Paris, and had embarked upon an intensive propaganda campaign involving the distribution of placards and hand-bills, the formation of special 'clubs' and the infiltration of the Government forces stationed in the city. The political message their agents preached was taken from that laid down in Babeuf's journal, and an attempt was also made to introduce an elementary programme for the training of cadres in techniques of revolutionary agitation. Lack of security ultimately led to the discovery of the plot and the death of most of those involved on the guillotine. Many years later, however, the originators of the 'Communist Manifesto' were to commend the Babeuvists as honoured predecessors, whilst later still Lenin was to mention them as being inspirers of the theories behind the formation of the Communist International in 1919.

But it was in the period of political ferment and renewed confusion that followed the fall of Napoleon and his empire, that the seeds of many of the tactics and methods of organization of the revolutionary organizations of our own day really began to be laid. Some of these organizations were concerned with the furtherance of revolution for the sake of social reform, others with its use for achieving national independence or freedom for some national minority.

One of the latter kind, with features of considerable interest, had come into existence even before the end of the Napoleonic wars, and was to have a considerable influence on the emergence of conspiratorial techniques. Known as the 'Carbonari', it operated in the kingdom of Naples and was devoted to liberating that state from the rule of the monarchy imposed upon it by Napoleon, whose first sovereign was the French Emperor's leader of cavalry, Murat. The organization of the Carbonari owed something to that of the Freemasons, to which a number of its members had belonged. It employed a curious ritual in which it made great use of symbols drawn from both Christianity and the trade of charcoal–burning. Operating as a secret society, it recruited nobles, army officers, small landlords, and even government officers and a few priests, and formed revolutionary cells all over the Kingdom. It appointed Jesus Christ as its 'Honorary Grand-master' who was always referred to as 'the Lamb' and new members had to swear to deliver 'the Lamb' from 'the Wolf', the latter representing the hated imposed monarchy.

Of all European governments one that had for long taken the most far-reaching measures against the dangers of revolution was that of Tsarist Russia. From the time of Ivan the Terrible onwards, governmental rule had been enforced and any sign of revolt ruthlessly crushed by a mammoth secret police force. The constant atmosphere of suspicion had bred a mania for secrecy at all levels of government activity, whilst the numbers employed in the service of the secret police or as informers ran into many thousands.

In 1825 this machinery of repression received and defeated a new challenge in the form of a group of aristocratic army officers who, drawing their inspiration from the American and French Revolutions, were bent upon forcing the Government to introduce some measure of social reform. Contact with the outside world during the Napoleonic wars had brought home to many young army officers and intellectuals just how far behind the rest of Europe their homeland was in all ways of life, and had resulted in growing pressure for radical change. The first secret society directed to this end had in fact been established in 1816 and was based partly on the pattern of Masonic lodges, to which some of its members belonged.

The activities of this society were to lead to the 'Decembrist' revolt in 1825, which was easily crushed in one day as it was merely the first episode in an almost continuous struggle that was to rock Imperial Russia for almost ninety years until the final overthrow of the régime in 1917. The totally unyielding attitude of many of those who led this régime was to persuade many, who at first based their hopes for the future on pacific reform, that the way ahead could in fact lie only through armed revolt; and was to breed an atmosphere in which conspiratorial work was to become almost second nature to many Russian intellectuals.

5

This strongly emerging strain of revolutionary thought was dominated throughout the first half of the century by 'the Populists', a strange variety of individuals, a few of whose names live on although most have vanished into obscurity. One of the former was Nicholas Gavrilovich Chernyshevsky, born in 1828, the son of an orthodox priest, and referred to by modern Soviet authorities as 'the great predecessor'. Adam B. Ullam, author of *Lenin and the Bolsheviks* writes of him:

> 'Chernyshevsky, below the veneer of extensive education and erudition that he acquired, is the typical Russian man of people. One finds in him a mixture of peasant slyness and of naïveté; of overpowering if at times sardonic humility, combined with arrogant self-confidence.'[2]

His belief lay in a kind of utopian socialism founded upon cooperatives, and the literary work for which he is most remembered is a political novel, *What is to be done?* The main message of this was the need for emergence of what he terms 'the new men', these being characters sure of their superiority to the common mass, but at the same time conscious of a mission to lead the masses to a better life, sacrificing themselves in the process if necessary. Chernyshevsky was not only a profound influence upon the radically minded, especially the young, of his own time but also on later revolutionary thinkers including Lenin.

One 'populist' group of considerable influence before it was broken up by the secret police in 1849 was the 'Petrashevsky Circle'. This included a group who called themselves 'Communists' and hoped for an early mass peasant rising, although its leader, Butashevich-Petrashevsky, favoured more a programme of preparatory propaganda and agitation direct to the 'masses'. Being himself from the nobility, like so many early Russian revolutionaries, he was very conscious of the need to get in direct touch with the people, and went so far as to join the 'Townsmen's Dancing Guild' purely in order to try to carry on propaganda amongst its members and make contacts. Mostly the circle operated in the form of a discussion group, and its importance was enhanced by its connections with great writers such as Fyodor Dostoevsky.

[2] Adam B. Ullam, *Lenin and the Bolsheviks*, The Fontana Library (London, 1969), p. 72

6

Despite all this growing activity, however, it does not seem to have been until the early 1840s that Russian revolutionaries began to devise a fully thought-out strategy of revolution. One of the first to do so was Nikolay Ogarev, collaborator and close personal friend of the leading revolutionary thinker Alexander Herzen. Like his friend, Ogarev had been inspired to thoughts of revolution by the 'Decembrist' revolt which had occurred in their boyhood, an event which caused them to swear an oath to sacrifice their lives working for the betterment of the lot of the Russian people.

Ogarev's theories on revolutionary action, which some authorities consider to have later greatly influenced Lenin's thinking, called for the setting up of an organization with two distinct roles. The first of these roles was the propagation of revolutionary theory; the second the construction of a strong underground organization based upon regional centres of population.

Below the regional centres Ogarev envisaged the revolutionary organization being extended by a network of local groups, the whole system being co-ordinated by a central headquarters and its agents. An interesting aspect of the scheme was his advocation of the use of what he terms 'unconscious agents', persons who could be used as auxiliary aides by being manipulated by revolutionaries without they themselves realizing that they were being so used. Not only individuals, but whole groups and organizations could be utilized in this way. He also recommended that members of revolutionary organizations should work their way into positions of responsibility, where they could obtain publicity as champions of the 'rights of the people'.

Ogarev was a great believer in the value of propaganda and drew up a comprehensive list of problems with which it should be designed to deal. His plans, which in the final stage called for armed revolt once the intelligentsia had been won over and a sound revolutionary organization constructed, were largely adopted by the revolutionary movement known as '*Zemla I Volya*', or 'Land and Freedom', which was active during the 1860s and 1870s.

In the early 1860s new and, in some cases, sinister strains began to appear in Russian revolutionary thought. Wearied of trying with scant success to transmit their thoughts to the uneducated and largely apathetic masses, a number of young revolutionaries began to speak of the need to build a secret organization

7

that would seize power and impose revolution on the majority of the population. A new breed of young fanatic began to appear, typified by Peter Zaichnevsky who headed a small group styling itself 'Young Russia', which issued a manifesto calling for the complete liquidation of the Royal Family and all those who were not on the side of revolution. He believed that 'any revolution afraid of going too far, is not really a revolution'. Although gifted with a genius for forming revolutionary cells wherever he went, he never attracted a large following, but some members of it survived to join ultimately the Bolshevik Party.

Zaichnevsky was far out-paced in fanaticism by a contemporary, Sergey Nechaev, the model for the central character in Dostoevsky's novel *The Possessed*. Of Nechaev it has been written:

> 'His personality and ideas portray, as if in a crooked mirror, the lust for revolution reaching even beyond political fanatacism into lunacy. With Nechaev we are already beyond Lenin, in the psychological atmosphere of conspiracy at once so grotesque and criminal as to forecast the darkest incidents of Stalin.'[3]

Nechaev left revolutionary circles in St Petersburg and went abroad to join forces with the anarchist Bakunin in producing a work entitled *Revolutionary Catechism*. According to the creed it laid down, a true revolutionary must forsake all other interests but work for the revolution, and must in fact become a 'lost man' with no morals or ordinary feelings. Everything was justified if executed in the name of the revolution, theft, blackmail, even murder. The *Catechism* included practical advice on how to carry out such deeds, and even gave approval to ordinary criminals as giving evidence of the revolutionary urges of the Russian people.

In 1874 there occurred an event which gave considerably greater weight to the view of those who believed that the masses must be coerced into revolution rather than gently led. This was the failure of the 'Pilgrimage to the People'. This had been conceived as a vast mission on the part of students and other young radicals from the cities to go into the countryside amongst the

[3] Adam B. Ullam, *Lenin and the Bolsheviks*, The Fontana Library (London, 1969), p. 104

peasants; partly to learn more about their actual conditions, but mainly to carry on propaganda amongst them to make them realize the wretchedness of their plight and aware of the need for and possibility of change. It was hoped that by helping the people with their day-to-day problems it was possible to convert them to radical views.

Everywhere the 'Pilgrimage' was an almost total failure. The eager young radicals found their presence at best barely tolerated and not infrequently openly resented, whilst their political message produced only bewilderment and confusion.

This rebuff to 'populist' theories of educating the people had drastic results. For to a number of hard-core revolutionaries it now seemed that if the people were not yet willing to listen to them, the only recourse they had was to strike directly at those they held most responsible for barring the way to progress, through whatever such violent means as they had at their disposal. As a result the 'Land and Freedom Movement' started to sanction the use of selective terrorism to eliminate especially reactionary provincial governors and 'traitors to the revolutionary cause'. Fundamentally the failure of the 'Pilgrimage' had done much to strengthen the hand of those who believed that only highly organized and centrally commanded groups could succeed in bringing about revolution, hand in hand with a greater acceptance of the views of such revolutionaries as Peter Tkachev, who held that coercive action was essential to revolutionary success; as were:

'speed, decisiveness and coordination of activities.' He also believed that only a minority could lead a revolution and that 'This minority in view of the higher mental and moral development always has and ought to have intellectual and moral power over the majority.'[4]

This point of view has in practice probably led to more shedding of blood than any other in recent history.

It was not long before the 'ultras' of the revolutionary movement came to regard the degree of terrorism being carried on by members of 'The Land and Freedom' movement as insufficient for their purpose, and formed a new organization, 'Narodnaya Volya' or 'People's Will', the main plank of its policy being

[4] P. N. Tkachev, *Collected Works* (Moscow, 1933), vol. 3, p. 223

redistribution of land to the peasants, and its main strategy the use of terrorism on a very much wider scale than anything seen before, in order to bring the establishment to its knees. Although 'The People's Will' never attracted more than 500 members or sympathizers at the outside and its hard-core activists consisted of only a few dozen persons grouped around 'The Central Committee', this tiny group succeeded in carrying on an intensive campaign of terror for over two years that shook the whole of the Tsar's vast domains. Its principal demand became the establishment of a Constituent Assembly through free elections. Its main target became the Tsar himself; after several attempts had failed members of 'The People's Will' finally succeeded in assassinating the relatively liberal Tsar Alexander II on 1 March 1881, the very day on which he had signed a decree which would have enabled elected representatives to sit in the highest organ of state. The immediate result was a new wave of reaction on the part of the authorities, which not only resulted in the crushing of 'The People's Will', but put paid to any more measures for evolutionary reform.

It is now time to briefly examine some of the more important events assisting the development of revolutionary thought and tactics that had been taking place in the world outside Russia. In 1848 there occurred the one that was in effect to prove of supreme importance for the long-term future. This was the publication of *The Communist Manifesto*, written at the special request of a newly formed and still largely unknown organization by the young Prussian revolutionary Karl Marx himself.

The Manifesto opened with the words: 'A spectre is haunting Europe—the spectre of Communism', and after maintaining that, 'all the powers of old Europe have entered into a holy alliance to exorcise this spectre: Pope and Czar, Metternich and Guizot, French radicals and German police spies', went on to state: 'it is high time Communists should openly, in face of the whole world, publish their views, their aims, their tendencies, and meet this nursery tale of the spectre of Communism with a manifesto of the party itself.'[5] Its main messages were in essence summed up in the lines near its commencement, which read:

[5] Karl Marx, *The Communist Manifesto*, Penguin Books (London, 1967), p. 78

* *

'The history of all hitherto existing society is the history of class struggles.

'Freeman and slave, patrician and plebeian, lord and serf, guild-master and journeyman, in a word, oppressor and oppressed, stood in constant opposition to one another, carried on an uninterrupted, now hidden, now open fight, a fight that each time ended, either in a revolutionary reconstitution of society at large, or in the common ruin of the contending classes.'[5]

Although Marx spent no more than six weeks' work on the manifesto, and although few people except Marx and his close friend Engels considered it to be a document of much importance at the time it appeared, the historian A. J. P. Taylor has summed up the enormous future importance of this virtual birth of the creed of Marxism by saying:

'Thanks to *The Communist Manifesto*, everyone thinks differently about politics and society, when he thinks at all. More than this, Marxism has become the accepted creed or religion for countless millions of mankind, and *The Communist Manifesto* must be counted as a holy book, in the same class as the Bible or the Koran. Nearly every sentence is a sacred text, quoted or acted on by devotees, who often no doubt do not know the source of their belief.'[6]

The first Communist organizations were rudimentary and possessed but a very scanty membership, some of them probably under a dozen. The first had the romantic sounding title of 'The League of the Just'. A few members of this body moved to London, where they formed a corresponding organization with the more plebeian title of 'The German Worker's Educational League'. It was to this body that Friedrich Engels introduced Marx. Marx was then himself living in Brussels, his political activities having made him unacceptable in his previous base in exile, Paris, where his first revolutionary writings had appeared in a short-lived review. In one of these articles he had outlined the thoughts that were to form the basis of his political philosophy. Disclaiming any belief in the possibility of any form

[6] A. J. P. Taylor, *The Communist Manifesto*, Penguin Books (London, 1967), p. 70

of partial political emancipation, he stated his belief that there was now only one class capable of carrying on a real and effective fight against authority and oppression—the proletariat, and in particular the industrial proletariat.

Marx approved of Engels' friends and their 'German Worker's Educational League', and himself established a similar group in Brussels, which he called 'The German Working Men's Association' whilst Engels tried to set up a parallel body in Paris. In addition to these groups Marx established a sort of co-ordinating body which was supposed to arrange liaison between the three feeble local organizations. This he first named 'The Communist Correspondence Committee', subsequently changing its name to 'The Communist League'. It was as the result of a meeting of this League in London that Marx was authorized to write *The Communist Manifesto*.

Many voices other than those of Marx and his handful of active supporters were, however, to command greater attention for many years yet, from amongst the ranks of the idealistic, appalled by the frightful and often deteriorating plight of the poor in many of Europe's cities, or the hopelessness of the lives of many of those condemned to eke out a bare existence from the land in conditions of semi-serfdom. Amongst these voices were those of the anarchists, and in particular those of such notable figures as Michael Bakunin.

Bakunin was the son of a noble Russian family, and when young entered the army of the Tsar. Leaving this profession he became involved in progressive Moscow literary and philosophical circles, and whilst still a young man went abroad, so becoming a travelling revolutionary and taking part in a number of unsuccessful revolts in places as far apart as Poland and Italy. He believed that immediate revolution by all categories of the underprivileged was essential for the solution of the world's problems, but did not believe that either prolonged preparation or organization was necessary for the success of such a revolution. Violently anti-semitic, he developed a feud against the Jewish Karl Marx, whom he came to regard almost as much an enemy as the Tsar, and in this feud lay some of the roots of the mutual antipathy that marks the relationships of Communists and anarchists to this day. He survived until the 1870s, ending his days in Switzerland.

Despite his aristocratic background he always considered himself a true representative of the people, and his teachings were among those that inspired young Russian intellectuals to go on the ill-fated 'Pilgrimage to the People'.

The anarchists of these times drew most of their support from poverty-stricken peasants, artisans, and students. They never succeeded in producing one single unified policy, and the attempts of Bakunin to form an Anarchist International ended in failure. The author of one study has said of nineteenth-century anarchism:

> 'Dispute and discord were of its very nature, it remained a collection of different emotions, ideas and actions, a broken mosaic of richly coloured pieces.'[7]

In the latter part of 1848, Karl Marx moved to Cologne where he soon became directly involved in attempts to foment armed revolt. These efforts, and the crushing of the revolution in Germany which broke out that year, were to lead to his expulsion, first again to Paris and then to London; where he was to spend the rest of his life, at first living in great poverty in Dean Street, Soho. Curiously Marx was not without some connection with Britain, as his wife, although the daughter of a high Prussian government official, was descended on her mother's side from the Duke of Argyll, executed by King William III for his part in Jacobite conspiracies.

In London Marx was to devote himself firstly to his literary work, and secondly to the masterminding of the activities of a body which represented the first really tangible effort to form an effective international revolutionary organization—'The International Working Men's Association' formed in 1864 and now generally known as 'The First International'.

Based for most of its life in London, it was dedicated to propagating revolutionary ideas including Marx's own developing theories through a number of branches on the continent; much of their activity being concentrated upon agitation in the young Trade Union Movement. Factional disputes led to the 'First International's' existence being but a short one and it was dissolved in 1873. Towards the end of its short life, however, an event occurred on which it had little if any influence, but which

[7] Roderick Redward, *The Anarchists*, Library of the 20th Century (London, 1971), p. 6

was to be of great importance in the development of revolutionary thinking: the French Revolution of March 1871.

The conditions which gave rise to this revolution had all the elements of a professional revolutionary's dream. Appalling social conditions, weak and ineffectual government, catastrophic military defeat, and national humiliation. From the practical point of view it was to demonstrate the inflammatory power of an extremist press and propaganda upon a population already under severe strain. All through that dark winter of 1871 and early spring of the next year, the beleaguered citizens of Paris were regaled with the violently anti-Government views of the extreme-left Press, including those contained in such organs as that edited by the well-known veteran revolutionary Blanqui, whose influence was a vital one amongst the extremists despite his absence in a Government prison, but above all by the paper which was to become the most savage mobilizer of revolutionary fervour, *Le Combat*.

Le Combat was edited by Felix Pyat, a sixty-year-old revolutionary who had spent most of his life in prison; a contemporary wrote of him as being: 'A distinguished man of subtle ideas and sensible speech, but as soon as he writes he becomes a madman, incapable of controlling himself.'[8]

The Press, however, was by no means the only medium of anti-Government propaganda, the so-called 'Red Clubs' playing a most important role. These institutions, which dispensed a programme of rough and ready satire combined with savage attacks on the authorities, became favourite haunts of the grossly swollen and largely idle 'National Guard', and they played an influential part in persuading many members of this force to transfer their allegiance from the Government to the revolutionaries, whose efforts were to result in the setting up of the short-lived but famous 'Commune' of the spring of 1871. An observer recorded at the time how readily the rank and file of the National Guard and their fellow citizens seemed to swallow the fare offered by the clubs, remarking:

'It is touching to see how these flocks of men are duped by the printed and spoken word, how marvellously deficient their critical faculty. The sacrosanct word "democracy" is able to fabricate a catechism even richer in miraculous

[8] Alistair Horne, *The Fall of Paris*, Pan Books (London, 1968), p. 136

14

fairy stories than the old one, and these people are quite ready to gulp it down devoutly.'[9]

The fearful and most bloody retribution exacted by the Government's forces after the collapse of the revolt was not only taken by revolutionaries throughout Europe as yet further proof of the basic inhumanity of the ruling classes, but was succeeded by a rising tide of indiscriminate violence on the part of the revolutionaries themselves. In the first wave of this tide were the anarchists, claiming the right to use violence as a matter of self-defence against the violence they claimed was habitual on the part of all those in authority. This new surge of revolutionary activity was urged on by the words of, amongst others, Prince Peter Kropotkin, like Bakunin a Russian nobleman who had turned away from his background to devote himself to revolutionary activities. He was to spend many years of his life living in exile in England.

A man of gentle character and a distinguished geographer, Kropotkin was none the less the most dedicated prophet of revolution, advocating: 'permanent revolt by word of mouth, in writing, by the dagger, the rifle, dynamite', and also declaring that 'everything is good for us which falls outside legality'. In his many pamphlets he denounced all authority as evil, and was responsible for coining the phrase: 'the urge to destroy is also a creative urge.'[10]

Anarchist activity had been mainly concerned with what in their own terms they described as 'propaganda of the word'. This in effect meant 'education' of 'the masses' as to the need for revolt. To the anarchist political armoury there was now to be added a second and sinister weapon, 'propaganda of the deed'.

Shortly after Tsar Alexander II was assassinated at the hands of 'The People's Will' in 1881, an event that was hailed with acclamation by many anarchists, an anarchist congress was held in a London public house where the delegates decided that 'propaganda of the deed' was to be encouraged. Although it was generally understood that such propaganda was to take the forms of practical acts of revolt that would draw attention to the

[9] Alistair Horne, *The Fall of Paris*, Pan Books (London, 1968)

[10] Roderick Redward, *The Anarchists*, Library of the 20th Century, (London, 1968), p. 13

revolutionary cause, its exact meaning was never defined. The term was, however, to be used as justification for a wide-ranging campaign of terror that was to continue into the early years of the next century and make the name 'anarchist' notorious.

The victims of this campaign were to include President McKinley of America and Empress Elizabeth of Austria, in addition to numbers of policemen, and a substantial number of unfortunate persons who just happened to be present when anarchist bombs exploded. Twenty persons were for instance killed in one bomb explosion in a Spanish theatre, and when a French anarchist student threw a bomb into a crowded bus station in Paris he expressed his disappointment at the result by saying: 'I wanted to kill and not just wound ... I hoped for fifteen dead and twenty wounded, unfortunately only one person was killed.'[11]

Not all anarchists supported this campaign of terror; of those who did many were obviously mentally unbalanced, such as the young man who killed the quite harmless Empress of Austria apparently merely because he wanted to kill someone so important that the act would get into the newspapers, or had criminal and somewhat grisly pasts, such as the French terrorist François Konigsten, alias Rauachol. Konigsten was not only a thief and forger, but before becoming involved in political terrorism had murdered an old hermit for the sake of his hoard of money, and on another occasion dug up a corpse in search of jewels. Despite this his execution resulted in his being hailed as a martyr by fellow anarchists and amongst them his revolutionary activities became a heroic myth.

Whilst the terrorist campaign achieved no practical results whatever, it did mark the birth of a strain of revolutionary thinking which is still very much with us today, and which can perhaps best be summed up in the words:

'Our modern civilization is a Moloch temple reared upon the bodies of slaughtered slaves. Let the terrorists do what they will, they cannot equal the crimes of our masters.'[12]

[11] Roderick Redward, *The Anarchists*, Library of the 20th Century (London, 1971), p. 41
[12] *The Anarchist*, quoted by Roderick Redward in *The Anarchists*, Library of the 20th Century (London, 1971), p. 48

CHAPTER II

The Technicians Emerge

For all their undoubted fervour there was a kind of amateurishness and haphazardness of action about most of the revolutionaries who came to prominence during the early and middle years of the nineteenth century. It was not until the century was nearing its close that a new breed of clear-thinking revolutionary tactician began to emerge, capable of reducing the process to an exact art, whereby repeatedly within the last sixty years or so originally tiny bodies of ruthless men have been able to overturn existing régimes and to impose their will upon the people of great or small states, democratic or non-democratic alike; or to reduce entire nations to long periods of turmoil.

Vladimir Ilyich Ulyanov, the son of an important Tsarist civil servant, who afterwards changed his name to Lenin, was born in 1870. When he was sixteen his elder brother was executed for his part in an alleged conspiracy to kill the Tsar, and Lenin himself became active in illegal socialist activity whilst still a young law student at St Petersburg.

It was not, however, until he was thirty-two and after years of banishment in Siberia and exile in various West European capitals, that his genius as a revolutionary tactician first became fully apparent. During his early years as an activist he had become convinced that one of the most effective forms of propaganda for preparing the ground for revolution was that of an underground newspaper. He saw such a paper not only as a means of getting the revolutionary message across, but also as an essential means of building an organization, maintaining that:

17

'A newspaper is not only a collective propagandist and a collective agitator, but also a collective organizer. In this respect it can be compared to the scaffolding which is erected around a building under construction.'[1]

Very soon after his release from exile in Siberia in 1898 he commenced the production of a new paper which he hoped would fill the role he had in mind, and was intended to unite all the revolutionary groups then at work in Russia.

The first edition of this paper *Iskra* (*The Spark*) appeared in 1900, and although few copies got past the border guards, eventually an efficient enough network of *Iskra* agents was established to ensure regular distribution of the paper through many areas of Russia. Lenin was himself a main contributor to the paper, which did much to enhance his reputation in revolutionary circles both inside and outside his homeland. For a short time he was aided in his work on the paper in his London base by a young fellow revolutionary who had recently escaped with his wife whilst on the way to exile in Siberia; and who to facilitate this escape had taken the name of his ex-gaoler, a name that was to become as well known as Lenin's own—Trotsky.

Lenin's widow has recorded a vivid picture of the devoted fervour, if somewhat primitive methods, with which the revolutionary exiles, moving from bases in shabby back-street lodging houses in one Western capital after another and awaiting with anxiety the midnight arrival of 'comrades' or couriers from the homeland, went about organizing the printing and despatch of propaganda materials for distribution by their agents in Russia.

'In London people immediately began to come and see us. We had a visit from Inna Smidovich ("Dimka") who soon afterwards left for Russia. Another visitor was her brother, Peter Hermogenovtich, whom, at the instance of Vladimir Ilyich, we christened "The Matron". He had just done a long stretch in prison. On his release he became a fervent "Iskra-ite". He considered himself a great expert at faking passports. He contended that the best method was to smear them with sweat. At one time all the tables in our "commune" were turned upside down to serve as presses for faked passports. The whole of this technique was extremely primitive,

[1] V. I. Lenin, *What is to be Done*, Panther Books (London, 1970), p. 207

18

as was all our secret work in those days. In reading now the correspondence carried on with Russia in those dark days, one marvels at the naïve form of our conspiratorial work. All those letters about handkerchiefs (passports), brewing beer, warm fur (illegal literature), all those code names for towns—beginning with the same letter as the name of the town ("Ossip" for Odessa, "Terenty" for Tver, "Petya" for Politiava, "Pasha" for Pakov, et cetera) all this substituting of women's names for men's, and vice-versa—all this was transparent in the extreme. It did not seem so naïve to us then, however, and did to a certain extent succeed in covering up the traces. In those earlier days agents provocateurs were not so abundant as they were later on. All our people were trustworthy and well known to one another.'[2]

A considerable variety of routes and methods of transport were used by the revolutionaries in their attempts to smuggle propaganda past the vigilant eyes of the Tsar's border police. Some of the material was despatched via a northern route via Vilna or Stockholm. In Marseilles a revolutionary agent arranged for the despatch of quantities in the care of members of the crews of ships sailing to the Black Sea port of Batum. In this case the practice normally was for the material to be wrapped in waterproof packages and dropped into the sea at pre-arranged spots just before the Russian coast was reached, later to be recovered by parties from the shore.

Austria was also used as a forwarding base, and suitable entry points were even sought along the Russian borders with Persia, the route in this case being via Cairo. Couriers sometimes carried propaganda literature with them in double-bottomed trunks or false bookbindings. Even so the exiles estimated that for a long time only some ten per cent of the material they despatched got through, although later a stage was reached when most of it was reaching its destination.

An increasing number of pamphlets and booklets as well as the paper were distributed by *Iskra* agents involved in the growing network in Russia, and some of these were reprinted there on illegal presses. One such publication was Lenin's *What is to*

[2] Nadezhada Frupskata, *Memories of Lenin*, Panther Books (London, 1970), p. 69

be Done, based upon articles of his which had previously appeared in *Iskra.* It was first published in 1902. It was to prove a work of the greatest importance, not only as far as the thinking and planning of the revolutionaries of the time was concerned, but also to this day in which it retains a high place on the obligatory reading list of many Communist party schools and courses.

Laying down important principles of organizational and propaganda work its pages stress the necessity of carrying on propaganda 'among all strata of the people', amongst whom its author considers revolutionary agents must go 'as theoreticians, as propagandists, as agitators, and as organizers'.[3]

Lenin, as he made clear in this work, believed that in order to win the cooperation of either individuals or groups of possible supporters, it was always necessary to appear as a champion of the particular cause which these particular potential recruits had dearest to their hearts; at the same time any such cause must always be made to seem related to the general one, the need for revolutionary change. For this reason he considered it essential for revolutionaries to be in advance of everybody else in taking up all matters of social discontent, and in exposing every possible example of Government brutality, corruption, or inefficiency.

Another point by which he laid great store was that to be successful a revolutionary party must contain a high proportion of 'professional revolutionaries' amongst its organizers and cadres; 'We must train people who will devote to the revolution not only their spare evenings but the whole of their lives.'[4] This was a point that was to take root with considerable effect, and even at the present time the number of full-time workers to be found in Communist parties is usually much higher in proportion to their strength than in other political parties.

Lenin always strove to impress upon his followers his belief that the revolution would be accomplished not by one single explosive act, but as the result of a series of upheavals and clashes that would continue over a prolonged period; he envisaged that the situation would alternate from 'more or less powerful explosions to periods of greater or lesser calm'. To meet such

[3] V. I. Lenin, *What is to be Done,* Panther Books (London, 1970)
[4] Ibid.

circumstances he was adamant that a comprehensive but at the same time adaptable form of organization was essential which would 'make use of everybody and everything', and be as ready to make swift changes of plan or disposition to meet changing conditions as any regular army in the field. Only an organization of this type, he argued,

'Will guarantee the flexibility which is necessary for a militant social Democratic organization—that is, varied and rapidly changing conditions of battle in an open field against an overwhelmingly strong enemy; on the other hand to make use of the clumsiness of this enemy and to attack him at a time when and at a place where he least expects attack. It would be the greatest mistake to build the party organization in the expectation only of an explosion and street fighting or only of the forward march of the grey, everyday struggle. We must always carry on our everyday work and always be prepared for everything, because very often it is almost impossible to see in advance the change from periods of explosion to periods of calm.'[5]

Lenin advocated that the ideal revolutionary party should consist of a Central Committee with, under it, two different types of subordinate Committees. The first group of these should be organized on a geographical basis and consist of area and local committees and in addition factory committees; considerable space in *What is to be Done* was devoted to the importance of the last and the methods by which their members should be chosen. The second group of subordinate committees should be of a 'functional'[5] or specialist nature, concerned with such matters as printing and publishing, transport, arms supply, manufacture of forged passports, counter-surveillance teams, mobile propaganda teams, trade unions, the organization of fighting groups, subversion of Government forces, and the running of commercial concerns to provide the party with funds.

In addition to these formal sections of the party organization Lenin also looked upon the formation of a number of auxiliary organizations as essential. The members of these, he believed, need not all belong to the party, but there must be at least one party member in each such group which, he recommended, should take the form of 'Workers' Circles' for the reading of revolutionary literature for 'self-education', and also 'Socialist or Democratic' circles which should be formed amongst members of all classes and occupations. The formation of such organizations should be 'everywhere' in the greatest possible numbers, and should have 'the most varied functions'.

Under Lenin's aegis Bolshevist propaganda developed into a two-edged weapon, propaganda and agitation; propaganda, or the detailed explanation of dogma and policy, being largely intended for the indoctrination of the more intelligent recruits to the party, whilst rank-and-file support was mobilized by means of what was openly termed 'agitation' around simple theories of class exploitation or matters of day-to-day discontent. This division has remained basic to Communist tactics.

By 1900 Lenin's followers had established a network of agents covering all the major Russian cities. Although Lenin himself remained in exile, he was able to make use of a number of reliable deputies who supervised the operation of this network. One of these was Leonard Krassin whose ostensible occupation was that of an engineer, but who also managed an illegal press and acted as a bomb manufacturer for the terrorist arm of the movement. The level of violence and internal strife swung sharply upwards in Russia after the failure of the 1905 St Petersburg rising, and it has been estimated that in the two years of 1906 and 1907 alone some 4,000 people lost their lives as the result of terrorism and political disorders.

In 1906 a new revolutionary paper edited by Lenin and named *Proletari* appeared, and the Bolshevist following grew to about 30,000. Six years later *Proletari* was itself succeeded by yet another paper which Lenin had in fact taken over from Trotsky's managership, and which carried a name which was ultimately to become world famous—*Pravda*.

By the time *Pravda* appeared on the scene as an all-Bolshevist paper, the stage had been largely set for that titanic clash of nations which was to see the techniques of propaganda and subversion used for the first time as major weapons of war, and which was to give rise to the growth of those two political systems, Communism and Fascism, which were to develop these techniques to a hitherto-unimagined degree and to blatantly use them for the enslavement of millions.

The outbreak of war found Lenin in Poronino, Austria, where he was arrested. However, a friend was able to intercede with an influential Austrian Socialist Leader, who secured his release on the ground that his anti-Tsarist zeal soon might be of use to the central powers, and he was allowed to depart for Switzerland which he reached in September 1914. Before long he was put into contact with a German-Swiss Socialist named Karl Moor, who was not only editor of a newspaper and a member of the Bern Great Council, but behind the scenes acted as a source of information for the German General Staff on leftist exiles living in his country. The outbreak of war, however, had been followed by a ferocious crack-down by the Tsarist police on Lenin's Bolshevist colleagues in Russia, and with his movement to a great extent forced to curtail its activities, Lenin's role as an active fomentor of revolution was to be considerably reduced in importance for the next three years, whilst other forces came to the fore.

These forces in the first place were provided by officials of the German Foreign Office, and members of the General Staff, who early in 1914 took a decision which was to have incalculable consequences for the whole history of Europe, and which marked the birth of a whole new dimension of war. This decision was simply to embark upon a large-scale programme of political subversion against their enemies, aimed not only at fomenting trouble for Britain and France in some of their colonial possessions; but also, more importantly, at dislocating the Russian war effort by promoting unrest in the Caucasus, the Ukraine, Poland, and Finland.

As summer turned into autumn that first year of the 'war to end war', the experts and agents engaged upon this scheme of subversion began to concentrate their efforts more and more upon a plan to subvert the Russian homeland itself; a turn which was to inevitably bring them before long into close contact with the scattered Russian revolutionary exiles. Strategically placed German Embassies in capitals covering routes into Russia were chosen as forward bases for the despatch of propaganda, agents and money. It was also decided that one of the main covers for the operation should be the introduction of a supposedly independent and liberal scheme for the 'liberation of oppressed peoples'; and to provide this with a plausible base a 'Fund for the Liberation of the Ukraine' was established in Switzerland.

This was the first of a number of such organizations set up to further the German plan; nominally independent, they were in fact tightly controlled from Berlin, and performed a most useful role for their German masters by acting as convenient agencies for the distribution of funds. It could in fact be said that they were the forerunners of the Communist-directed front organizations which perform such important tasks for their Soviet and Chinese masters today.

From early 1915 the scope of this scheme of subversion was to be greatly enlarged, as the result of the appearance on the scene of one whose aid was to prove utterly invaluable to the German masterminds in charge of it. Alexander Parvus (who also used the name of Helphand) was one of those extraordinary and somewhat mysterious characters with whom most writers of fiction would hesitate to strain their reader's credibility, and yet who not so infrequently have a considerable, sometimes immense, influence on the course of events.

By birth he was a Belo-Russian and became converted to Marxist theories very early in his life. During the attempted revolution of 1905 he established a reputation for himself as one of the leading theoreticians of the revolutionary movement. Subsequently arrested and sent to Siberia, he managed to escape and went to Germany where he became a publisher and literary and theatrical agent. He later became interested in the increasingly restive political situation in the Balkans and moved to Constantinople in 1910.

Using the Turkish capital as his base, he not only busied himself with Social-Democratic propaganda activities directed at neighbouring states, but also developed a large and highly profitable import-export business, his merchandise reputedly including obsolete German arms. Travelling widely through the area, he used the political and economic knowledge his travels brought him to the very best advantage, and became a figure of influence and power. As financial adviser to the party of the 'Young Turks' he set to work to persuade his Turkish friends that it would be in their country's best interests to enter the war on the side of Germany.

Parvus's support for Germany was based not on sympathy for her imperial ambitions but on his admiration for German Marxists and his belief that a German victory could be utilized to produce a spreading revolution, commencing in Russia. He now approached the German authorities with an offer to foment revolution in Russia whilst the war was still in progress, through a carefully prepared scheme which he titled 'Preparations for a Political Mass Strike in Russia'. The essence of this was the use of a tactic which has since become fundamental to the revolutionary agitator seeking to secure support from amongst industrial workers: the launching of strikes apparently to secure economic objectives, but in fact to encompass political demands. Eventually, after these political demands had mounted to the extent of a call for the replacement of Russia's rulers there would be a general strike, which should, he thought, result in the collapse of the Government. Parvus envisaged that agitation should be largely concentrated upon the St Petersburg area, and in particular upon three large factories within it. He also proffered advice for the raising of mutiny in the Black Sea Fleet, large-scale sabotage and the smuggling of arms and ammunition.

Not surprisingly it was not long before German diplomats and soldiers were convinced that in Parvus they had a man of whom they could make good use. He was given a German passport and authority to set about putting his plan into effect. To enable him to make a start the German Treasury was ordered to make available to him the sum of 2 million marks for propaganda in Russia.

Parvus established his headquarters in Copenhagen, hiding its real purpose under the name of an innocuous sounding 'Scientific Institute', ostensibly engaged upon economic and social research to aid in postwar reconstruction. To staff this headquarters he recruited a small number of Russian revolutionaries living in Switzerland, amongst them Lenin's friend Fürstenberg-Ganetsky. At first the entire staff consisted of only eight people, these directing the operations of ten agents actually inside Russia. With his usual energy, however, Parvus soon greatly extended his activities, setting up a web of commercial companies run by cover men in Denmark, which augmented his own fortune and brought funds for the use of the 'institute'; for the same purpose he also engaged in large-scale black-market trading.

Before long a revolutionary newspaper, *The Bell*, was being produced and taken into Russia by a regular service of couriers.

Parvus estimated that it would take some 20 million roubles to really get a revolution started in Russia, and a problem arose as to how to find sufficient sums in Russian notes, and also how to get the money safely into Russia in order to pay agents and meet their expenses. To solve these problems, Parvus used methods which have been used many times since. Alan Moorehead has described how:

> 'Parvus tackled this matter with his usual flair; he entered into business with Russia. All through this period the Russian borders were loosely controlled, and the Russian regulations for trading with the enemy had many loopholes ... specifically they allowed the import into Russia of many German metals, including copper, iron, steel, aluminium, nickel, tin and lead. Parvus entered into this trade on a large scale, and even expanded the range to include electrical goods and such medicines as salvarin which under false labels and by other means were shipped to Petrograd. A part at least of the roubles he collected was left in Russia and distributed to the revolutionary cells by his agents there.'[6]

Moorehead also describes Parvus as one who had an aura of money 'hanging over him'. Quite how much of the funds he received in the course of his clandestine activities found their way into his own pocket is unknown, but it is certain that after the war he settled in Switzerland with a personal fortune of 30 million Swiss Francs.

In addition to the activities directed by Parvus the German plotters themselves had not been idle. A special secret 'Bureau for the Russian Revolution' was opened in the Wilhelmstrasse, working closely with the High Command and the Foreign Office. The printing presses of the Admiralty were brought into service to produce revolutionary literature for despatch into Russia, and

6 Alan Moorehead, *The Russian Revolution*, Panther Books (London, 1958), p. 131

more front organizations established. Nor was Parvus's by any means the only network of revolutionary agents employed, although his seems to have been considerably the most effective. Another leading agent to obtain importance was Alexander Keskula, an Estonian Bolshevik with a devout admiration of Lenin's organizational abilities, to which he was to draw his German backers' attention.

By early 1916 tangible evidence began to appear that the German-sponsored revolutionary campaign was taking effect. The number of strikes in Russian industry was multiplying, and increasingly the demands of the strikers began to assume a political nature, as well as being for higher wages and better working conditions. Although obviously the German authorities involved and the revolutionaries took the most elaborate precautions to cover up their mutual connection, this became well known to the Russian security services and Government Ministers and was an increasing source of worry.

Although the campaign was put into low gear for some months after the middle of 1916, as the result of growing fears in the Wilhelmstrasse that revolution would merely result in the establishment of a Liberal-Socialist Government pledged to continue the war on the allies' side, it was hastily revitalized after the February revolution of the following year, which taking most by surprise so quickly toppled the Government and brought about the abdication of the Tsar. But it led to the establishment of precisely what the Germans had come to fear—a moderate provisional government willing to continue the war. Before long the Foreign Office was requesting the sum of 5 million marks for renewed propaganda inside Russia. Now German hopes were to become directly centred, with the most dire results for world history, upon promoting the Bolsheviks as the revolutionary element most certain to take Russia out of the war once in power.

The attention of the German Government and High Command had already been drawn to Lenin in his Swiss refuge much earlier by both Parvus, who never got on well with him, and by his admirer, Keskula. Both men had reported on his possible usefulness on account of his known opposition to the war. Parvus had visited him in 1915 but had been refused any assistance by Lenin, who afterwards told his followers not to have anything to do with Parvus's 'institute', but Lenin must presumably have been kept constantly informed of its operations by his close friend, Fürstenberg-Ganetsky.

The German High Command now, in Sir Winston Churchill's words, 'turned upon Russia the most grisly of all weapons. They transported Lenin in a sealed truck like a plague bacillus from Switzerland into Russia.'[7]

By the time Lenin actually reached the Russian border via Finland, the German subversive propaganda machine had already been at full blast again for some months. A German agent and newspaperman had been installed in Petrograd with the sum of 3 million roubles and instructions to set up a pro-German newspaper. These operations were supported by a base organization in Stockholm from which funds were paid into agents' accounts in Petrograd. Alan Moorehead states that German records clearly show that money was paid to the Bolshevists in Petrograd in substantial amounts, from March 1917 right up to the outbreak of the final revolution in November that was to bring Lenin and his colleagues to power, and which in turn resulted in the eastern armistice by then so desperately desired by the Kaiser's High Command.

Lenin had, in fact, almost been as much taken by surprise by the outbreak of the February Revolution as everyone else. Shortly before, he had been expressing his belief that he and his contemporaries were unlikely to see the revolution in their lifetime, and his first reaction on the unexpected news reaching him from Petrograd had been to declare his belief that the sensational events were the result of a plot on the part of the French and British Embassies to forestall a separate peace between Russia and Germany. But since the true state of affairs had become clear to him, he had been in a fever of impatience to return home. On 3 April he finally dismounted from the train at Petrograd's Finnish station to a hero's welcome and a military band playing the only revolutionary anthem it had yet had time to learn, 'The Marseillaise'.

Lenin's Bolshevik followers had only played a small part in the events of February, and although they had been granted two

[7] Alan Moorehead, *The Russian Revolution*, Panther Books (London, 1958), p. 175

seats on the Executive Committee of the Central Council of Soviets, which had established the provisional Government, this was more of a token gesture on the part of the 'bourgeois' revolutionaries who now governed Russia than any mark of respect for what little influence the Bolsheviks were thought to wield.

The prospect, though, for the professional revolutionary who had written *What is to be Done* to put tactical theory into full practice could hardly have been better. Nearly four years of war and 5 million casualties had left the army demoralized and near-broken, and soon 2 million deserters were to be roaming the country. The weak and divided Government of Kerensky had been unable to deal either with the food shortage or soaring inflation, and was rapidly digging its own grave by allowing more and more power to pass into the hands of local Soviets; and by even further relaxing the already extremely shaky discipline of its armed forces.

Lenin had already decided the main lines of his attack upon the Government he intended to destroy before his return, and one of these became apparent the very day of his arrival. 'The alleged defence of the Fatherland means the defence of one band of capitalists against another,' he declared to the welcoming crowds, and from that moment the main Bolshevik propaganda line became one of thoroughgoing opposition to the war and encouragement to the front-line troops to fraternize with the German and Austrian enemies. To this was also added another increasingly popular call, which in later years was to become the refrain of many another Communist revolutionary. The solution of the 'Land Programme', declared Lenin, lay in the confiscation of all estates and the redistribution of the land among the peasants. Still another slogan used with great effect by Lenin's followers was that of 'All power to the Soviets', the Bolsheviks not being one wit disturbed by the practical absurdity of the thought that these loosely-knit local revolutionary councils could provide a stable framework of government. Lenin's eyes were already stretching far beyond the frontiers of Russia and all his thoughts were bent on the destruction of the bourgeois Provisional Government by a Bolshevik-led revolution which would touch off a train of others across Europe. The question of a proper form of government for Russia could come later.

29

By the end of May the Bolshevik propaganda campaign had already resulted in a number of army units passing under Bolshevik control; to his impatient subordinates, who urged that now was the time to strike, Lenin replied: 'We are now in a minority. The masses as yet don't believe us. We shall know how to wait.'[8]

On what would seem a suicidal impulse the Government now rescinded all regulations forbidding political activity within the army, and freely allowed the passing of propaganda amongst its members. The Bolshevik propaganda effort amongst the troops was stepped up and a special paper, *The Trench Pravda*, produced for distribution in the now crumbling front line. The military section of the Central Soviet condemned the Bolshevik anti-war activity, but it was decided to take no action against them as long as they confined themselves to 'peaceful propaganda'.

In July the Bolshevik party, which at Lenin's order was shortly afterwards to change its name to 'Communist', held its sixth congress; its membership had increased from some 50,000 in April to over 240,000; and it was much better organized than other parties in the field, with most of its members concentrated in the two focal cities of Moscow and Petrograd. In June, however, it had suffered something of a setback when its call for massive demonstrations against the Government by members of the army was frustrated by unexpectedly firm action on the part of the Central Soviet. It had now become fully clear to Lenin that the time of preparatory propaganda and agitation was drawing to a close and that action must come soon. Accordingly the slogans on the banners, posters, and leaflets began to change to 'Power can no longer be taken peacefully', and 'All power to the Revolutionary Proletariat'.

The Bolsheviks, sometimes working with ultra-left socialist allies, were now busy trying to capture control of the various Soviets and in September were successful in Petrograd and soon afterwards in Moscow. At the same time an increasing number of army units were also falling under their domination. Trotsky was appointed chairman of the Petrograd Soviet, and in October a 'Military Revolutionary Committee' was established under its

[8] Adam B. Ullam, *Lenin and the Bolsheviks*, Fontana Library (London, 1969), p. 439

auspices, ostensibly to defend the city against the rapidly advancing German forces, but in reality to act as a common organization to take charge of the far-advanced Bolshevik preparations for armed revolt.

The final decision to act was taken by the central Committee of the Party on 10 October, not without considerable argument, and not a little misgiving on the part of some members. Many of the Bolshevik leaders had grave doubts about their followers' martial qualities, and gloomily feared that many of them would run away if any had the temerity to actually open fire on them. It was the fiery and vigorous Trotsky, who was to act as Commander-in-Chief of the insurgent forces, who now reinfused all concerned with the proper degree of revolutionary fervour. The rising was to be directed in Petrograd by a three-man committee, whilst Trotsky and Lenin were to remain at a headquarters located in a former girls' finishing school in the town of Smolny.

The revolt was planned to begin on the night of 23 October with the seizure of the Winter Palace, seat of the Provisional Government, but a chance encounter between the detachment of Red Guards detailed for this task and a squadron of Government cavalry forced a forty-eight-hour postponement. Whilst Trotsky assured the Smolny Soviet, which was led by non-Bolshevik elements, that all talk of an imminent rising was greatly exaggerated, the unfortunate Kerensky was announcing to his Governmental colleagues that at last he felt he had sufficient proof of Bolshevik ill-intention to take effective action against them, only to become bogged down in endless argument. The last preparations were being made and Lenin, who for some time had been forced to live an underground existence in hiding, went disguised and wearing a wig to join Trotsky in the completely unprotected revolutionary headquarters in the old finishing school.

The operation that night proceeded smoothly on what have since become, from frequent repetition, classic lines. By dawn all the strategic points in the city, bridges, telephone exchanges, power stations, had been occupied. No resistance was met, and in the afternoon followed the almost equally unresisted but much fabled 'storming' of the Winter Palace, wherein were assembled the members of the Provisional Government except Kerensky, who had left the city on an unavailing quest to gather loyal

31

forces. On the afternoon of the following day the end of the Provisional Government was announced to members of the Central Soviet by Lenin and Trotsky, the former ending his speech with the words: 'Long live the worldwide socialist revolution.'[9]

In such manner did the party which had been formed eleven years before by a small group of dissidents begin to impose its will over the peoples of one of the greatest countries on earth; and to achieve its first safe base from which to launch its continuing crusade for world mastery: a crusade which might be said to have first begun to take practical shape less than two years later, with the formation of its first main instrument, 'The Cominform'.

The next practitioner of the art of revolution, who was to contribute most to its rapidly developing evolvement, was hardly one of those to whom this clarion call from the Third International was addressed.

In March that same year at a poorly-attended meeting in Milan was formed the Fascist party, which only four years later under the leadership of Benito Mussolini was to seize power from the hands of the inept Italian Government of the day.

The son of a father who had first been strongly attracted towards anarchism and had then turned to socialism, Mussolini's early political career before the outbreak of war had been concentrated upon work for the Socialist party, and writing for and editing its publications. In the articles he wrote in those days the young Mussolini made frequent reference to his admiration for Karl Marx, describing him as the 'father and teacher'. He became convinced both of the absolute correctness of Marx's teaching that the 'privileged class' would not give up its privileges without being forced to do so, and of the whole Marxist theory of class war. Accordingly he came to increasingly believe that no worthwhile change could be brought about without revolution; and that revolution could only succeed, as Marx advised, as the result of the most careful preparation.

Even some time after the outbreak of war Mussolini was such a devotee of Marx that he could be found writing:

[9] Adam B. Ullam, *Lenin and the Bolsheviks*, Fontana Library (London, 1969), p. 486

32

'The red flags planted on the Galician trenches have the highest symbolic value. It is the revolution which does not fear war, it is the war which rescues the revolution. The flags with the Imperial eagles; they will not withstand the red flags of the revolution. The Red Flag will rise on the Palace at Potsdam too when the armies of the revolution and of the Western Democracies have shattered the Germany of the Hohenzollerns and of Shieman.'[10]

The last words of the above quotation betray the rising anti-Germanic feeling, ironic in the view of later events, which for a time was to become an obsession and cause him to distrust all those Russian revolutionaries, including Lenin, who in any way used German support. During the war too his thinking changed to the belief that capitalism had a long life ahead of it, and consequently he came to dismiss many of Marx's teachings from his mind; although he retained his belief in the necessity for revolutionary change.

The party formed as the result of the Milan meeting was headed by two committees, the first of which was known as the 'Commission for Propaganda', and included Mussolini himself as one of its members. With the country repeatedly hit by strikes and violent political disturbances, often Communist-inspired, and social discontent rampant, a party which spoke out strongly in favour of the restoration of order combined with a degree of social reform, and supported the introduction of a strong nationalism with which to combat the 'decadence' and 'rottenness' of the times, stood a sound chance of being listened to. At the founding meeting a decision had been taken to build up a party organization covering the whole country with a network of *fasci* or propaganda groups. The new movement made good progress and by the end of the year could claim a membership of 40,000, controlled by some 200 *Fasci*. For some time the new party's most effective propaganda weapon was its paper *Popolo d'Italia*, which also functioned efficiently as a 'collective organizer'.

In the spring of 1920 the first party strong-arm squads made their appearance, first formed in Trieste and known as 'Action Squads'. They were recruited from the most suitable members

[10] Ernst Nolte, *The Three Faces of Fascism*, R. Piper Verlag (Munich, 1963), p. 229

33

of local *Fasci* groups. Equipped in the first place with somewhat amateurish weapons, they nevertheless soon developed an efficient system of cooperation which enabled them to take rapid action on their own initiative; in some places the squads became accepted by strife-weary local populations as something of an unofficial militia or police. Each Squad had its own name chosen carefully because of its historical connections, and its own standard, of which the central motif was usually the lictor's bundle or the death's head. The uniform members of these squads wore soon gave them their name of 'Blackshirts'.

As party organization improved small *Fasci* came to be formed wherever there were more than twenty party members. Each *Fasci* had its own political secretary, and all local groups were under the immediate control of Provincial Federations. The 'Action Squads' came to be divided into two sections, one providing its first line strength and the other reserves. The Government placed no hindrance in the way of sympathetic army officers who wished to help the development of the party's 'military arm', and in command at its apex sat a general.

Special party organizations were also established for women, students and youth. Members whose employment was in the public institutions or public services were enrolled into bodies known as the *'Gruppi di Competenza'*, the main role of these being strike breaking. Members of the 'Action Squads' were supposed to perform their duties in what was described as a spirit of 'profound mysticism' and blind obedience to orders. Mussolini felt that:

> 'Democracy has deprived the life of the people of "style" that is, a line of conduct, the colour, the strength, the picturesque, the unexpected, the mystical; in sum, all that counts in the soul of the masses. We play the lyre on all its strings; from violence to religion, from art to politics.'[11]

Encouraged by the growing strength of his party and the lack of effective opposition, Mussolini removed all restriction on the actions of its military arm from 1922 onwards. As a result whole districts rapidly became virtually under the control of the party, its rule being enforced by the 'Action Squads' who often

[11] Ernst Nolte, *The Three Faces of Fascism*, R. Piper Verlag (Munich, 1963), p. 331

34

expelled all those who did not support its policies from the area, burning their homes. The squads made great use of motor transport and so-called 'fire columns' were despatched in wide-ranging forays as mobile arsonists to attack the property of political opponents or that of the Government. Shooting, beatings-up, and massive purging with castor oil were also favourite techniques employed by the Fascists to spread terror and intimidation. Even the cities provided no safe refuge against the increasingly bold attacks of the 'Action Squads'. In the summer of 1922 a Blackshirt force of many tens of thousands descended on Bologna and camped in the streets for weeks like an army of occupation.

With the country subjected to such a prolonged and large-scale campaign of propaganda and intimidation, it is not surprising that the march on the capital by the Fascist legions was virtually unresisted and so culminated in the Party's triumph.

The success of Mussolini's adroit use of propaganda and agitation combined with the use of force ruthlessly employed made a profound impression upon that fast-learning German revolutionary, Adolf Hitler; whose own movement at the time of Mussolini's victory was still just emerging from the status of a miniscule fringe group. Hitler had always been a great believer in the power of propaganda, and his biographer, Dr Alan Bullock, has written that his genius as a politician lay in realizing what it could accomplish and seeing how best to put it to work.

Hitler's basic ideas on propaganda betrayed not only the most arrogant contempt for his avowed enemies and opponents, but also an almost equal contempt for those 'masses' of the German nation whom during his rise to power he sought to recruit as his followers. In a typical passage he wrote:

> 'The receptive powers of the masses are very restricted and their understanding is feeble. On the other hand, they quickly forget. Such being the case, all effective propaganda must be confined to a few bare necessities and then must be expressed in a few stereotyped formulas.'[12]

His same underlying disdain for the people over whom he wished to gain influence is evident in his remarks regarding the use of lies in propaganda; assessing the greater credibility of big lies than of small lies he explained:

[12] Adolf Hitler, *Mein Kampf*, Hurst and Blackett (London, 1939)

35

' ... that in the big lie there is always a certain force of credibility; because the broad masses of a nation are always more easily corrupted in the deeper strata of their emotional nature than consciously or voluntarily, and thus in the primitive simplicity of their minds they more readily fall victims to the big lie than the small lie, since they themselves often tell small lies in little matters, but would be ashamed to resort to large-scale falsehoods. It could never come into their heads to fabricate colossal untruths and they would not believe that others could have the impudence to distort the truth so infamously ... The grossly impudent lie always leaves traces behind it, even after it has been nailed down.'[13]

Hitler also believed that propaganda must be aimed at exploiting the emotions of those to whom it was addressed rather than at carrying any deep intellectual message:

'The driving force which has brought about the most tremendous revolutions on this earth has never been a body of scientific teaching which has gained force over the masses, but always a devotion which has inspired them, and often a kind of hysteria which has urged them into action.'[14]

It was not the written word but 'the magic power of the spoken word' upon which Hitler was most to rely to produce the hysteria which he sought to sweep him to power. Throughout its rise to power the basic propaganda weapon upon which the party relied was the party orator and the fulminations of the local agitator. The Nazi propagandist never scrupled to exploit the desires or fears of the ambitious, the envious, or the embittered in every class, regardless of their known character, in order to gain recruits of influence. Habitual drunkards, perverts, pimps, even murderers and blackmailers, all were welcome additions to its ranks so long as they could be made good use of, and in not a few cases such individuals soon achieved high rank and position in its hierarchy, consequently soon giving it the well-justified reputation of containing more shady characters than any other party in Germany.

Despite Hitler's and his lieutenants' oft-repeated claim during

[13] Adolf Hitler, *Mein Kampf*, Hurst and Blackett (London, 1939)
[14] Ibid., p. 283

the party's rise to power in the years after the failure of the 1923 Munich Putsch, that 'the party had stood rock-hard upon legality' and had no intention of seizing power by violent means, it was always evident that the Nazi Party intended to use the democratic machine merely to carry out a revolution by destroying the democratic constitution once power was safely in its hands, and so achieve a position of despotic, unchallengeable authority—very much the tactics that many Communist parties were to come to adopt in later years.

Apart from the Jews, the bitterest hatred contained in Nazi propaganda attacks was directed against the parties of the centre and moderate right and moderate left, or all who stood for the maintenance of democratic government and opposed revolutionary solutions to the country's problems. All these elements without exception were accused of treachery during or since the War, corruption or decadence. Although he was later to make great play with the claim of having saved Germany from Communism, Hitler made it clear on more than one occasion in his early days as Party leader that he in fact viewed the Communists with much more sympathy and respect than he did his democratically minded opponents.

'In our movement the two extremes come together: the Communists from the left and the officers and students from the Right. These two have always been the most active elements, and it was the greatest crime that they used to oppose each other in street fights. The Communists were the idealists of Socialism.'[15]

On the domestic front the party claimed to represent 'the little man' and to uphold his interests against interference from big business. But the main and most vital emphasis of the propaganda machine was on the allegation that all Germany's troubles were due to treachery at home and unfair treatment abroad, a line well-attuned to the psychological needs of a population smarting under the humiliations of military defeat and economic depression, and who in the words of one commentator of the times were only too apt to 'pray not only for their daily bread but also for their daily illusion.'[15]

[15] N. S. Briefe, No 23 (June, 1929), quoted by Alan Bullock, Hitler, A Study in Tyranny, Odhams Press (London, 1952), pp. 160-1.

A belief in the effective use of violence and fear had always been basic to Hitler's political thinking. Dr Alan Bullock has said that in this regard he hit upon a psychological fact which was to prove to be of the greatest importance: that as propaganda displays of physical force tend to attract as many as they repel. Hitler openly believed in the constant employment of violence as a political weapon. Very early in his career he set about creating a force which could be used for this purpose, and which was to prove its worth again and again on his road to power.

This force sprang from the strong-arm squads recruited to guard party meetings and at first camouflaged under the name of 'Gymnastic and Sports Division'. But before long they were given a title under which they were to become notorious, the *Sturmabteiling*, or SA. From the start their role was offensive as well as defensive. Operations upon which they became increasingly employed including the breaking up of political opponents' meetings, it being a set principle of Nazi policy to 'ruthlessly prevent—if necessary by force' all meetings or lectures which, as Hitler put it, were 'likely to distract the minds of our fellow countrymen'—words that have found a curious echo in the utterances of some Marxist revolutionary students of present times.

A large-scale recruiting campaign for the SA was begun, many new recruits coming in from the 'Free Corps' and other private armies of the same type that had been active in Germany after the armistice. As with the party in general, 'suitable' recruits were admitted regardless of their pasts. The Commander of the Munich SA, for instance, Lieutenant Edmund Heines, not only had a notorious record as a homosexual but had actually been convicted of murder. The SA were formed into 'Hundreds', of which there were eight by the end of 1921. Ultimately it was to grow to a force of 400,000 spread over the entire country.

A party machine was steadily built up which had the dual aim of subverting the power and morale of the state, and of providing a niche in which every section of the population sympathetic to the Nazi Party's aims could be made to serve the cause. This machine was divided into two main compartments. The first, known as PO1, had as its main task the undermining of the Government and existing social order, and included amongst its sections both those dealing with foreign affairs and with trade unions. The second, PO11, had sections dealing with such matters as agriculture, economics, justice, and 'race and culture'. Also under its jurisdiction came special sections for students, teachers and civil servants, doctors, lawyers and jurists. A special *Kulturbund* was formed to attract intellectuals, and for the rising generation aged between 15 and 18 there was the Hitler Youth with its own propaganda, 'defence sports', press, culture and other departments. For those of even younger age there was the *Deutsche Jungvolk* which catered for those between 10 and 15, and two other special organizations, one for girls and another for women.

Administratively the party organization was divided into thirty-four districts or *Gauen*, each more or less corresponding with the thirty-four electoral districts of the Reichstag, and each under the direction of a *Gauleiter* directly responsible to Hitler. The next lowest unit of organization was the *Kreise*, or circle. At the bottom of the chain came local groups of supporters which in large urban areas were sub-divided into street cells.

In the early years the Party's propaganda machine was under the direct control of Hitler himself, but in 1927 he handed over this control to a young Party official whose name will for ever be assured of a high place amongst the exponents and practitioners of the art of revolutionary propaganda and agitation— Joseph Goebbels.

Like his leader, Goebbels in the early days of his political career had more than once expressed some sympathy for those he was later to spend so much time denouncing as his country's arch-enemies, the Communists. Shortly after joining the Nazi Party he was still writing in his diary that it would be better to end up under Bolshevism than to 'endure slavery under capitalism', and lamenting what a terrible thing it was that his Nazi comrades and the Communists should be 'bashing in each other's heads'. In 1925 he even published an open letter in which he assured a Communist leader that in reality Nazism and Communism were exactly the same thing, and that the two, although then in opposition to each other, were not real enemies.

His ideas on the use of propaganda were clear cut; its task was not to entertain but to produce results and in essence it was 'nothing but the predecessor of an organization', an organization

39

which in itself would be the predecessor of a new state. His views on the value of the use of force differed in no important respect from those of Hitler. He firmly believed that whoever could conquer the streets would one day conquer the state. Consequently, he declared, there could never be enough public demonstrations organized by the party; every form of power politics had its roots in such demonstrations, which were the most concrete assertion possible of the party's will to govern; they were much more important than election statistics, for thousands of men marching up and down the streets were in effect taking part in nothing less than a 'mobilization for power'.

Holding such views, Goebbels made the greatest possible use of the SA for propaganda and publicity purposes. He employed its units in carefully staged attacks upon opposition political meetings, and organized boycotts of Jewish shops and provocative marches through areas where their presence was bound to result in clashes with the Communists and others. Every possible ounce of publicity was squeezed out of the funerals of any members of the SA killed in the course of such operations, and they were always attended with the most elaborate party ceremony intended to build up the image of the SA as being both heroes and martyrs.

The attack of the Nazi Party upon the Weimar Republic also took the form of a campaign for the subversion of the whole life of the nation, and a detailed exploitation of all social divisions, grievances and prejudices, for which, as an example of revolutionary technique, Lenin could have had nothing but the highest praise. This campaign was described by one of Hitler's leading supporters:

> 'Everything that is detrimental to the existing order has our support ... We are promoting catastrophic policies— for only catastrophe that is, the collapse of the Liberal system will clear the way for the new order ... All that serves to precipitate the catastrophe of the ruling system, every strike, every Governmental crisis, every disturbance of the state power, every weakening of the system—is good, very good for us and our German revolution.'[16]

[16] *N. S. Briefe*, No. 23 (June, 1929), quoted by Alan Bullock, *Hitler, A Study in Tyranny* (London, 1952), pp. 160–1

Despite the mammoth scale of the Nazi Party's propaganda effort and campaign of intimidation, for many years the Party never attracted the support of anything but a small minority of the electorate. Given the scale of this attack and the immense fervour with which it was pressed, however, it was almost inevitable that in the end events were to follow so exactly the path Hitler had sketched in a letter written to a colleague, whilst still in prison after the disastrous and undignified failure of his 1923 Munich coup.

'When I resume active work it will be necessary to pursue a new policy, instead of working to achieve power by armed coup, we shall have to hold our noses and enter the Reichstag against the Catholic and Marxist deputies. If outvoting them takes longer than outshooting, at least the result will be guaranteed by their own constitution. Any lawful process is slow ... sooner or later we shall have a majority, and after that, Germany.'[17]

In the case of both Italy and Germany the path of the subversives who were to destroy democracy was undoubtedly eased not only by the manner in which weak and indecisive governments had failed to face the challenge of previous Communist-inspired violence and subversion, so losing public confidence, but also by the failure of such governments and moderate political forces to appreciate the growing dangers until it was far too late.

[17] Kurt Ludecke, *I Knew Hitler* (London, 1938), pp. 217–18

CHAPTER III

The Coming of People's War and Wars of Liberation

It soon became apparent that the hopes of the leaders of the victorious Russian revolution, that their own success would swiftly lead to a spate of similar revolts throughout Europe, were doomed to as much disappointment as had been the sort of expectations held by the French revolutionary leaders before them.

As early as 1921, repeated disappointments in Germany and elsewhere had shown clearly that the overthrowing of the world capitalist system was going to be a long and complicated business; and accordingly plans began to be directed more and more to the carrying out of a protracted war of attrition against it.

Part of these plans included the setting up of special training schools inside the Soviet Union for picked cadres from the outside world, from which it was hoped would emerge the revolutionary leaders of the future. One of the first of these to be established was specially intended for students from the Far East, known as the 'University of Toilers of the East'; it included Ho Chi Minh amongst its pupils.

The syllabus at these schools included both the Marxist classics, *What is to be Done* and works by Lenin, and also newer studies by active participants in the revolution based upon their own experiences. The message in these was always much the same: the need for thorough and complete preparation in every field before any revolutionary attempt was launched.

In 1920 a special conference was held in Baku on the Black

Sea to decide on Communist policy towards the peoples of the colonial territories and other areas outside Europe. From this conference stemmed a shift in Communist policy that was to have the most important effects. It was decided that the Communist cause was most likely to prosper in such regions not through efforts to start openly-led Communist revolts, but through a skilful exploitation of existing nationalist and anti-colonial sentiment; and the support by Communists of even the most bourgeois type of nationalist leader. The ending of colonialism must be the first step; indoctrination of the masses over whom it had held sway could then follow.

A year later, at the Comintern Conference of 1921, an important directive on the future of Communist tactics was presented in the form of a thesis written by Lenin himself.

The emphasis in this thesis was on the assiduous use of propaganda. Communist propaganda and agitation, Lenin wrote, must everywhere be implanted in 'the very midst of the workers'. It should be carried on through three main channels: 'Verbal propaganda', by word of mouth, active work in trade unions or political organizations, and the party press and mass distribution of literature. Lenin laid down that every single member of a Communist party, either legal or illegal, should, without fail, regularly take part in one or other of these methods of propaganda. Emphasis was also put on the need to carry out intensive agitation amongst members of national minorities where these existed, as well as for Communist workers in industry to carry on a 'regular personal agitation' in the workshops, together with the distribution of literature.

In addition, Lenin laid stress on the advantages to be gained by making use of such organizations as educational boards, study circles, sporting clubs, dramatic societies, consumers' associations, and war victims' associations, all bodies of such a type, he said, could form useful 'transmission belts between us and the workers'.

After seven years of hard work nurturing the efforts of the inexperienced Communist parties that had sprung up across the world, the Comintern produced another highly important directive at its sixth congress in 1928, a directive which again has great relevance to continuing Communist policy. It stressed the need for Communist parties to take up and support even the most insignificant demands of the people, gradually changing and moulding these demands into major ones for sweeping and revolutionary change; and linking them finally to the need for the establishment of Communist power.

As the years passed and the chances of successful armed revolt in Europe seemed to dwindle, the directives of the Comintern began to lay more stress on the strategy of the 'united front'. This would give to Communist parties the opportunity to gain power through constitutional means, then to destroy the capitalist system and the democratic machinery of government, and to usher in the revolution with the authority of the state at their disposal.

Meanwhile, with as great a significance for the future, the seeds of another element were already bursting into life. The Communist Party of China had been founded at a secret meeting in the French concession in Shanghai in 1921. The previous year the Russians had sent two emissaries, one a Dutch Communist, to sponsor the formation of the new party. The founding meeting was small, consisting of cell leaders from various parts of the country; amongst them a young man who had founded a cell in Hunan, Mao Tse-tung.

At the time of its formation the party only had fifty members, and three years later had still only grown to a strength of about 400. Throughout its early years it was dominated by a Politburo which was under tight Comintern control, and Soviet influence dominated its policy-making. The orders it received were to concentrate upon agitation in the cities and towns, and upon gaining influence amongst industrial workers in preparation for urban-based revolution.

But it was not long before Mao Tse-tung began to show disagreement with this policy. Even before the party had been formed he had had considerable experience of revolutionary work, and had given much time to the study of its strategy and tactics. Although he acknowledged the importance of work in the cities, it was the peasants, he felt, that offered the most promising material from which to forge a revolutionary army. In 1927, his first major chance to prove his worth came when he was ordered to raise an armed revolt in his home province of Hunan. The

venture was a total failure, and with his ill-armed force completely routed he himself only narrowly escaped capture.

Mao Tse-tung proceeded to lead a ragged and dejected band of
1,000 survivors to a remote area of pine-covered mountains on
the borders of Hunan and Klangsi provinces. This unauthorized
action drew the ire of the Politburo, from which he was dismissed. At this time his force had only 200 rifles between its
members and its future prospects seemed indeed dim.

Almost immediately, however, its leaders embarked upon a
calculated programme to rebuild its morale. He had become convinced that no dependable revolutionary army could be created
unless its members were thoroughly indoctrinated as to its aims
and policies. Accordingly he introduced a programme of intensive political education which was to become the hallmark of
Asian Communist guerrillas in future years. There was a Communist Party cell in every section, the lowest sub-unit of the
force, a party branch in each company, and as the strength of
the force grew special party committees were established at
battalion and regimental level. Political study sessions were held
around camp fires in the evenings and formed part of the normal
training syllabus by day.

In the early days of this nucleus of what was to become the
Chinese Red Army, the proportion of party members to non-
party members was maintained at a level of one to three; later it
was raised to a standard one to two.

Mao Tse-tung did not confine the activities of his small force
to training and study. Raids began on the territory of local landlords, and a system of redistribution of land to the peasants was
instituted. These early operations taught him yet another important lesson. The local peasants seemed far less receptive to
the new ideas his followers tried to impart than he had expected;
thus impressing on him the need for a successful revolutionary
army not only to fully indoctrinate its own members, but also to
be ready to carry on intensive propaganda amongst the people
wherever it went to enroll their support.

From this unpromising start commenced a period of more than
twenty years of almost uninterrupted guerrilla warfare against
both Government forces and Japanese invaders, which in the end
was to make Mao Tse-tung not only master of China but also the

acknowledged master of that blend of propaganda, psychological warfare and violence which has become known throughout the world as People's War, and which has served as a model for many of the revolutionaries of the last two decades.

As indicated previously, one of the main lessons learnt by Mao Tse-tung in the long campaign in China was the vital need for revolutionary guerrillas to both control the population amongst which they operate, and to obtain the maximum possible support from it. His answer to the problem of achieving these results largely lay in carrying out what he termed a 'political mobilization'. The necessity for this became a central point in his teaching, and in his military writings he explained:

'What does political mobilization mean? First, it means telling the army and the people about the political aim of the war. It is necessary for every soldier and civilian to see why the war must be fought and how it concerns him. . . . How should we mobilize them? By word of mouth, by leaflets and bulletins, by newspapers, books and pamphlets, through plays and films, through schools, mass organizations, and through our cadres. . . . Our job is not to recite our political programme to the people, for nobody will listen to such recitations; we must link the political mobilization for the war with developments in the war and with the life of soldiers and the people, and make it a continuous movement.'[1]

Mao Tse-tung has said that such propaganda activities should be conducted by tens of thousands of trained cadres and hundreds of mass leaders. At the same time the winning over of the mass of the people should not be left only to normal propaganda methods, and revolutionary guerrillas should also be willing to engage in more practical measures in order to gain support along the following lines:

'We must go among the masses; arouse them to activity; concern ourselves with their weal and woe; work earnestly and sincerely in their interests and solve their problems of salt, rice, shelter, clothing and childbirth. The women want to learn ploughing and hoeing (so we unexpectedly discover). Whom can we get to teach them? Children want to

[1] Mao Tse-tung, *Selected Military Writings*, Foreign Languages Press (Peking, 1967), p. 221

go to school (or at least we encourage them to want to go to school). Has any primary school been set up? The wooden bridge over there is too narrow (although the villagers did not realize this). Should not repairs be made? All such problems concerning the living conditions of the masses should be placed on our agenda. [In such ways] we should make the broad masses realize that we represent their interests, that our life and theirs are intimately interwoven.'[2]

The problem of finding the correct methods of ensuring mass support for revolutionary activities was also to attract much thought from other later revolutionary leaders, such as Ho Chi Minh and General Giap, Fidel Castro and Che Guevara. The last was to declare that the revolutionary guerrilla should regard himself as also being a social reformer, saying:

'The peasant must always be helped technically, economically, morally, and culturally. The guerrilla fighter will be a sort of guiding angel who has fallen into the zone, helping the poor always and bothering the rich as little as possible in the first stages of the war ... The guerrilla fighter as a social reformer should not only provide an example in his own life but he ought also constantly to give orientation in ideological problems.'[3]

Despite such idealistic sentiments, and despite Mao Tse-tung's strictures on the need for good behaviour and humane treatment of civilians, campaigns of recent years have made it very clear that in practice modern revolutionaries in arms will not hesitate to resort to other methods of obtaining the public support so essential to them, if peaceful persuasion and gestures of aid to the local population should fail. These other methods are coercion in the form of selective terrorism and intimidation. The manner in which gentle methods of persuasion and terror have been used together in a closely interwoven combination by revolutionary guerrillas of the post-war years deserve close study.

RECRUITMENT OF REVOLUTIONARY FORCES AND THE SEARCH FOR SUPPORT FROM THE MASSES

The leading counter-insurgency expert Sir Robert Thompson

[2] Mao Tse-tung, *Selected Works*, Volume I, pp. 135–7
[3] Che Guevara, *Guerrilla Warfare*, Penguin Books (London, 1969), pp. 46–7

has said that recruits to Communist revolutionary movements in arms are of three main types.[4] Firstly come the 'naturals', those persons who see little future for themselves in existing society, such as those who may have failed important examinations or have had trouble with the law, and having a grudge against society they wish to change it so as to be able to demonstrate the talents they profoundly believe they have and which they think have so far been unrecognized. The second category consists of the 'converted', those who may have suffered from Government abuses of power, or been persuaded into joining the movement by friends already within it, and also those who think that the revolt is likely to succeed and want to join the 'bandwagon' early so as to assure their futures. It may also include members of Government forces who have decided to change sides.

The 'deceived' category comprises members, often young, who have been gradually drawn in after having first been recruited into political discussion groups, or some form of completely legal political social work directed by those of whose true motives they have no idea. A situation is then 'developed', involving those who have been recruited into such front organizations in some confrontation with authority, thus embittering them against the existing wielders of power, and so reducing them into a suitable frame of mind for recruitment into the revolutionary movement itself.

An interesting example of the manner in which young recruits can be drawn into the service of a revolutionary movement, by what might be described as a process of 'slow seduction', has come from Thailand.

The story concerns a young Thai from the Ubon Province of Thailand, the son of a moderately prosperous rice paddy farmer. The young man greatly desired to become a doctor. One day his father was approached by a friend who said that he had heard his son was an intelligent boy, and that he would like him to join him in his business of selling noodles. The young man, Bunkong, and his father felt that this was a good opportunity and accepted the offer. Bunkong took up residence with his father's friend Mr Mun and found that the latter seemed to have a considerable

[4] Sir Robert Thompson, *Defeating Communist Insurgency*, Chatto and Windus (London, 1972), pp. 35–6

interest in his future plans. On hearing that Bunkong eventually hoped to become a doctor, he said that only the sons of rich men in Bangkok stood any chance of becoming doctors, and that Bunkong could not expect to get any help from the Government in obtaining training who, he was told, were not interested in the problems of poor people and were imposing unfair restrictions and taxation upon them.

He himself, Mr Mun said, had studied medicine in a 'faraway land' which had a good government willing to spend a lot of money on the people's education. Sometimes this government was willing to give training to people from foreign lands which suffered under bad governments. The time came when Bunkong was asked if he would like to go and study himself in this 'faraway land'. When he said that he would he was told that first he must read many books and study hard. Mun then gave him a succession of books to read on such subjects as the suffering of Thai youth under the 'maltreatment' of the existing government, and on how there was no chance of a better life under the present system of administration.

Later Mun took Bunkong to several small meetings organized by the Communist Party of Thailand. These were held in the rice paddies or just in the jungle; between eight and ten persons were normally present, and the meetings were usually held at night. Mun was sometimes one of the speakers at these gatherings, his favourite target for attack being the presence of American troops in Thailand and American imperialism. Strong criticism of the Government was also made and gradually Bunkong began to feel a real hatred for both the Government and for the Americans.

After some time Mun told Bunkong that it would now be possible for him to go to the distant country he had told him of, where he would be able to train as a doctor. In January 1965, Bunkong and a number of other would-be trainees set off on a journey that ended not as he hoped in a medical college, but in the Political and Military Training School of the Communist Party of Thailand in North Vietnam. Here he was given instruction intended to fit him for the role of guerrilla in his own country.

Communist parties engaged or preparing to take part in 'armed struggle' still maintain a high level of theoretical political study

49

and training, and go to considerable pains to maintain large libraries, even under the most unfavourable conditions, to help them do so. Amongst papers discovered by police investigating the activities of the Communist underground organization in Sarawak was a library list of 273 works dealing with politics, history, economics, and 'self-cultivation', and oddly a section on fiction and poetry.

A police search in another part of the country was the means of the discovery of a carefully concealed library of some eighty books including Marxist classics, books on guerrilla warfare, philosophy, and science. This library was divided up and buried in polythene bags at scattered points in a jungle area. Members of the organization wishing to borrow books from the library had to do so through an intricate lending scheme, which avoided any borrower being brought into direct contact with the key man of the whole system, the librarian.

Quite often when a Communist party goes underground and takes up 'armed struggle' some sort of front organization will take over its overt political function. New recruits to the movement will have to first serve a probationary period with the front organization before being sent on to the training camps in the guerrilla base area if considered suitable material. In the training camps political studies are given almost as much attention as military training, and normally include group study of Marxist works and self-criticism sessions, in which the recruits have to confess any faults or failings in front of all their comrades.

The political commissar, or political officer, is an invariable part of the establishment of all Communist guerrilla forces, and is often represented in the command structure of even small sub-units of the force. His function is to advise the military commander on all political matters, and he has charge of the political education of all members of the unit to which he belongs. Normally he has equal seniority with the military commander and they are supposed to take all important decisions in conjunction.

The political commissar system has also sometimes been copied by non-Communist revolutionaries and 'Freedom Fighters'. In Algeria, for instance, political officers attached to all units played a most important part in the campaign. They were usually men of considerable political experience and some had served in the

French army or worked in France. As well as being responsible for the political education of the FLN guerrillas they were also responsible for maintaining good relations between the guerrillas and the Arab civil population. They were constantly on the move from village to village, sometimes accompanied by a doctor, and possibly two nurses, and a secretary.

Their duties involved the forming of FLN cells in every village in their area, and the organization of a system of local Government in areas under rebel control, particularly the appointment of local officials and tax collectors. In theory a tenth of the income of every man in an FLN area went to swell the movement funds. The political officers also organized a rough and ready social security system, and arranged for the setting up of schools staffed by members of the FLN. A system of 'people's homes', usually in fact caves, intended as refuges for members of the movement who had to pass through or work in disputed areas, provided the political officers with convenient local bases near each village from which to operate.

A similar system of political officers was used by the Egyptian-backed National Liberation Front in Aden; here their main task was to indoctrinate members of the movement with the principles of Arab Socialism as propagated in Cairo.

Revolutionary movements in arms often had very much more difficulty than they have ever admitted in both finding recruits to join their ranks and in obtaining that degree of mass support that is essential to their success. The picture of whole segments of a population eagerly rushing to aid the revolutionary cause, which revolutionaries so like to present, would seem in fact to be a rare occurrence. In Algeria the FLN had a perpetual and severe recruiting problem which became so grave that it had to be met by the introduction of conscription in areas under its control. (In Vietnam the Viet Cong was forced to introduce similar measures.) Threats had to be made that action would be taken against the families of deserters in order to check defection, and at the beginning of the campaign the FLN was in addition faced with the general apathy, if not hostility, of the great bulk of the Muslim population.

To counter this, in December 1955 the FLN set in motion a special propaganda campaign designed to win 'the minds of the

Muslim people'. Large numbers of FLN agents were sent out among the people to explain the movement's revolutionary aims, to persuade, and to intimidate. This intensive campaign which lasted for three months met with encouraging results and from then on the FLN began to get a firm grip on the population. It continued to pay great importance to propaganda, and a special propaganda and psychological warfare section formed part of the headquarters of each *Wilya*, as the FLN's area commands were known.

Farmers' associations and peasant leagues are frequently used by revolutionaries in undeveloped countries as fronts for recruiting the nucleus of a guerrilla force in outlying districts. The organization of fund-collecting cells, composed primarily of young people, the more promising of whom are gradually transferred to more secret and dangerous work, is another well-known recruiting tactic; it was in use by the forerunners of the Viet Minh and the Viet Cong, the Communist Party of Indo-China, as early as the late 1920s.

At a recent seminar held under the auspices of the South East Treaty Organization in Bangkok, it was concluded that the main pattern of Communist activity at the commencement of an armed revolt in more primitive areas was as follows:

1 The despatch of cadres to areas where there are good grounds for discontent.

2 The setting up of revolutionary organizations among the peasants.

3 The provoking of conflicts between peasants and land-owners and the incitement of the assassination of government officials, thereby involving as many people in breaking the law as possible.

4 The creation of leaders out of those who have played a major part in ambushing government forces and carrying out assassinations.

5 The prosecution of a propaganda campaign to persuade the peasants that they need defence forces to defend themselves against government forces.

6 The establishment of a secure base area in the jungle or mountains, from which to operate and make forays against centres of population and government outposts.

7   The linking together of the base areas by expanding the areas of influence around them.

In the area of the Thai-Malaysian border, the Communist guerrilla force known as the Malayan National Liberation Army, which suffered complete defeat during the twelve-year campaign in Malaya that ended in 1960, has been showing signs of preparing for new efforts. It has been involved in a vigorous drive to obtain popular support from the inhabitants of the three Thai provinces in which it has taken refuge, largely through a programme of social welfare work. Members of the Liberation Army have taken part in nursing the sick, helped to organize old people's benevolent associations, and provided the local population with drugs. They have also taken part in anti-malaria work and sent entertainment troupes to brighten the monotonous existence of the villages isolated in the jungle.

Their area of operation is inhabited by a mixed population of Thais, Chinese and Muslim Malaysians. The Liberation Army has produced considerable quantities of propaganda designed to appeal to Muslim opinion, of which the central theme is that those who join the Liberation Army and fight with it against imperialism are in fact being true to the Prophet Mohammed's philosophy and commands. The Liberation Army also produces equal amounts of propaganda directed at the Buddhist section of the population, and in this the message is that in fighting against imperialism and neo-colonialism the Liberation Army is following the principle of Buddhism by practising good deeds and eliminating evil. Help has been given to the Muslim community in building mosques, and prayer mats and joss sticks have been provided for Buddhist worshippers.

In some cases Communist guerrillas have made special attempts to attract the support of members of aboriginal tribes in areas in which they are operating. During the campaign in Malaya, specially selected cadre party members were sent on missions deep into the jungle to contact the aboriginals who lived there, and get their cooperation. They were instructed to make their approach with 'sympathy and love' and to let it be known that they respected the aboriginals' customs, even though other people might despise them. In order that this approach might be really effective they carried out a deep study of these customs and rituals. Some of the guerrillas even adopted the aboriginal style of living, wearing nothing but a loincloth and going barefoot. They helped the aboriginals improve their methods of crop production and provided seeds and implements. They instituted a health service. Eventually they won the aboriginals' confidence sufficiently to organize them into 'self-defence units', which in turn produced some guerrilla fighters. This effort was so successful that in 1953 it was estimated that the great majority of the deep-jungle aboriginals had been brought under Communist influence.

Both the Viet Minh and the Viet Cong have used similar tactics in attempting to attract the support of primitive tribes in Vietnam. The commander of the former, General Giap, stated that a swearing-in ceremony was usually necessary to secure the allegiance of such recruits.

A sustained effort to gather support and generally create a favourable impression by means of social welfare work is now a standard procedure in the early stages of a Communist-led insurgency in undeveloped countries, and is quite often also carried on in conjunction with the military campaign, once this has begun. In Sarawak, Chinese members of the Communist organization preparing for armed action who lived in the towns learnt hairdressing and became travelling barbers and hairdressers, moving from one Dyak longhouse to another, providing a welcome service for the people; but most importantly they could provide themselves with excellent opportunities to glean information and to get to know the people's desires and complaints.

The establishment of a rudimentary health service and the teaching of hygiene have become two of the most common 'services' provided by Communist guerrillas engaged in enlisting support for a coming campaign. Particular emphasis has been placed on this form of activity by a number of Latin American guerrilla groups.

The immense care taken by members of some guerrilla forces, engaged in assessing the possibilities of support from different sections of the population, can be seen from the fact that the report of one Communist cadre in Sarawak included a list of almost the entire Chinese population in the district in which he worked, with an 'ideological rating' given against each name.

To the Communist guerrilla, and an increasing number of

other modern revolutionaries, armed action and propaganda are not viewed as two different aspects of the fight, but as a single element in which both have equal importance, and they are to some extent interchangeable, in that armed action is frequently used for what are essentially much more propagandist than strategic or tactical purposes, and propaganda is often used to disrupt and demoralize enemy forces in a manner which the guerrillas' lack of strength would bar them from doing by purely military means.

Revolutionary guerrilla forces often produce very large quantities of propaganda literature, either in their own base areas or across the frontier in some friendly country where they have a sanctuary. Not infrequently they are also equipped with their own mobile radio transmitter, an increasingly potent weapon with the enormous rise in the number of receiving sets in the homes of even the poorest countries, thanks to the arrival of the transistor.

The revolutionary guerrilla's favourite propaganda weapon in the developing countries of the Third World still tends to be the 'armed propaganda team', which first made its appearance in Indo-China with the Viet Minh and whose function has been defined as follows by Regis Debray:

'... The first nucleus of fighters will be divided into small propaganda patrols which will cover the mountain areas, going into villages, holding meetings, speaking here and there, in order to explain the social goals of the Revolution, to denounce the enemies of the peasantry, to promise agrarian reform and punishment for traitors, etc. If the peasants are sceptical, their confidence in themselves must be restored by imbuing them with revolutionary faith; faith in the revolutionaries who are speaking to them. Cells, public or underground, will be organized in the villages; union struggles will be supported or initiated, and the programme of the revolution will be reiterated again and again. It is only at the end of this stage, having achieved active support by the masses, a solid rearguard, regular provisioning, a broad intelligence network, rapid mail service, and a recruiting centre, that the guerrillas can pass over to direct action against the enemy.'[5]

[5] Regis Debray, *Revolution in the Revolution*, Penguin Books (London, 1968), p. 46

AGITATION AMONG YOUTH

One of the endless prodding exhortations that Lenin used to send to his fellow conspirators in Russia from his various bases in exile was 'Go to the youth, Gentlemen, otherwise, by God, you will be too late'; and the greatest importance has been attached to agitation and organization amongst young people ever since those days, both by Communists and other types of revolutionaries.

One of the most interesting examples of subversive activity being carried on amongst young people by Communists, with the aim of building a revolutionary organization, comes again from Sarawak.

In 1951, Teo Yong Jim, a young Chinese school teacher from Sarawak, visited Singapore and there came into contact with a Communist front organization known as the Anti-British League; and through this organization was put in touch with the urban branch of the Communist Party of Malaya, whose task was to give clandestine support to the guerrillas in the jungle. Returning to Sarawak, he at once set about trying to establish a Communist revolutionary organization in that country. He began unifying various radical discussion groups in which he had previously been involved, most of whose members were also school teachers, and forming them into a body which he named the Sarawak Liberation League.

At the time there was considerable fruitful ground for the growth of a subversive movement in the schools that catered for the children of the large Chinese population, as there was then a general feeling that the opportunities for Chinese in the country were extremely poor, and that the educational facilities provided for them were far from adequate. The new movement grew rapidly within the schools, where it was based upon a three-member cell system. Separate cells existed for teachers and pupils, and all recruits had to serve a probationary period before becoming accepted as full members of the League and swearing an oath of loyalty to it. By the end of 1954 there were about nineteen cells and the organization had a total membership of about 100 people.

Members were expected to take part in concentrated study, either by themselves or in groups, of the writings of Marx and

56

Lenin, but at the same time it was emphasized that their activities should not be restricted to mere theory. Study should be followed immediately by practical action in the form of agitation within the school, and in expanding its network by helping establish cells in other schools where they did not yet exist.

The majority of active members were senior pupils, and when the time came for them to leave school they were told to make full use of the political training they had received in any way they could in their working life. All were instructed to join the trade union appropriate to their job, and to try and ensure that they gained some sort of position of responsibility within it as soon as possible. Some of the more dedicated Communist-indoctrinated pupils deliberately went into jobs where they felt they could make their political influence felt to the greatest extent possible, such as on the staff of Chinese newspapers or in the teaching profession. Others obtained positions on the governing boards of Chinese schools or as school secretaries. Gradually members of the Sarawak Liberation League began to dominate groups such as the teachers' associations and old school associations.

One group of Liberation League members made a particular point of carrying out agitation amongst teachers in the countryside; and as a result the league's message before long began to find its way even into the smallest village and hamlet school. By the close of 1956 most of the important trade unions in the country's three main towns of Kuching, Sibu, and Miri were under Communist control. At some time around 1956, a special additional organization was set up under the direction of the Liberation League, but with the particular task of directing agitational work in the schools; its title was the Sarawak Advanced Youth Association. Two years later the influence of the two organizations had grown so much that the nucleus of a revolutionary organization had already been well-established.

Intense agitation amongst youth has continued as an integral and essential part of the preparations being made by Sarawak Communists for armed action, preparations which have been causing the Government of Malaysia increasing concern.

The report of one cadre which fell into the hands of the police showed clearly that primary schools had also become targets for agitation and attempts at recruitment. The report stated that the cadre concerned had recruited fifteen 'youths', some of these recruits being as young as eight and still at primary school. Another captured report spoke of a girl of twelve being particularly suitable for use as a courier because of her 'political innocence'. In some areas recruits from amongst primary school pupils have been formed into special small children's groups. Some propaganda leaflets have been directed at persuading parents to let their children join in revolutionary activity, which is described as 'an immensely happy and glorious undertaking'.

A revolutionary movement of a completely different type of political motivation that also made great use of the recruitment and organization of young people to assist its activities was EOKA. General Grivas has himself said that from the outset of the campaign in Cyprus he attached the greatest importance to the creation of a youth movement:

'The use of young people in a battle of this kind was entirely my own idea. I know of no other movement, organization or army which has so actively employed boys and girls of school age in the front line. And yet there is every reason to do so: young people love danger; they must take risks to prove their worth . . . I began the youth organization by appointing an agent in each town: his task was to choose a leader at every school, who would, in turn, set up class leaders. There was a separate organization for youths of school age who were working.'[6]

School children were constantly mobilized to take part in anti-British demonstrations, and one of the first large-scale events of the kind took place on the 24 May 1955 when some 700 children attacked police. Grivas has boasted that after that nothing could hold the school pupils back and that they learned to act in 'blind obedience' to his orders. He has put on record his conviction that this organized use of school children was one of the chief factors which resulted in EOKA's ultimate victory, saying that British troops were baffled when they found that bomb throwers were 16-year-old schoolboys or that leaflet distributors were 10-year-old primary school children.

Primary school children were in fact brought into the battle as

[6] Grivas, *The Memoirs of General Grivas*, Longmans, Green (London, 1946), p. 29

the result of a direct order from Grivas that the Greek flag should be flown and kept flying from all primary schools. A special organization for mobilizing schoolgirls to take part in street demonstrations was also formed. Grivas makes it clear that all this was not accomplished without some resistance from the Cypriot school authorities and that he had 'severe action' carried out against certain 'incorrigible teachers' who resisted his plans.

TERRORISM AND PSYCHOLOGICAL WARFARE

The American authority on the Vietnam war, Douglas Pike, has written:

'It is more difficult than might first appear to distinguish between terror and violence or between terror and war. Terror of course is a pejorative word, one which each side uses to depreciate the activities of the other. Without being too far afield, it would seem fair . . . to define terror as illegal violence, assuming that warfare although immoral in ethical terms, is legal in the context of international law, but that even in warfare certain acts are illegal and may properly be termed terror. This latter point rests on the belief that in all things there are limits, and a limit in warfare is reached at the systematic use of death, pain, fear, and anxiety among the population (either civilian or military) for the deliberate purpose of coercing, manipulating, intimidating, punishing or simply frightening into helpless submission. Certain acts even in war are beyond the pale and can only be labelled as terror.'[7]

There is ample evidence to show that terrorism as defined above has been deliberately used as a major weapon in their armoury by many of the insurgent movements of the post-war years, especially, although not exclusively, by those under Communist control.

It would of course be pointless to deny that on occasion acts have been committed by government forces engaged against insurgents that could justly be described as the use of terror; but in general these have usually been the result of indiscipline amongst units of security forces or the unauthorized action of

[7] Douglas Pike, *The Viet Cong Strategy of Terror*, United States Mission, Vietnam, p. 2

59

local commanders, rather than deliberate policy. Although extreme brutality against rebels on the part of authority may have been the rule rather than the exception in the past, most modern democratic governments have come to realize that the use of such measures in counter-insurgency operations is not only inhumane, but also highly counter-productive. Modern revolutionaries on the other hand would seem to be placing an ever greater reliance on the use of terrorism.

For them terrorism has three main roles, of which the first is propagandist; the explosion of a bomb in a crowded shop near some city centre or the throwing of a grenade into the market place of some village or provincial town may seem pointless from the military and tactical point of view. To the revolutionaries who planned it, however, the point lies purely in the explosion and the subsequent reporting of its effects. It is propaganda of the deed in its most drastic form: causing shock and bewilderment and illustrating in practical form that a dissident movement in arms undeniably exists, and has the power to strike at targets of its choice. Such random acts of terrorism, whose purpose is purely to announce the arrival on the scene of a dissident movement in arms, have become increasingly common in the early stages of an insurrection. Quite often they will be continued for a protracted period whilst the insurgents are gathering strength for more major attacks, in order to ensure that news of their existence percolates not only throughout the country concerned but also around the world. If the movement continues to lack sufficient support and strength for major military ventures such tactics may become its main means of expression, as has been the case with the Irish Republican Army's campaign in Ulster.

The second aim of the use of terrorism is to destroy those elements in the population who may take the lead in opposing the revolution, and all those servants of the Government upon whom it particularly relies, especially members of the security services particularly concerned with counter-insurgency; but also members of the civil administration down to quite low levels, and members of professions upon whom the fabric of normal society depends, such as teachers and doctors. Terrorism of this type would seem to be becoming an increasingly inseparable part of Communist revolutionary activities in developing countries, and is sometimes carried out with appalling thoroughness—as in Vietnam.

The third role of terrorism is intimidation, aimed either at coercing the civil population into support for the revolutionaries, or at frightening it into refraining from doing anything which might harm the revolutionaries or their cause. Terrorism used for this dual purpose has become a main weapon of insurgents in practically all revolutionary campaigns of the post-war period.

Terrorism made its appearance early in the campaign mounted by the Communist ELAS forces in Greece from 1945 onwards. First came a programme of liquidation of 'uncooperative elements', and later a campaign aimed at adding to the Government's already enormous refugee problem. This took the form of raids on villages bordering the edges of areas under Communist control, the pillaging of most of the villagers' goods, quite frequently the massacre of many inhabitants in order to induce the remainder and those in surrounding villages to flee. Terrorism was also used in Greece to persuade the population to give practical aid to the Communist forces. In some cases orders were given that one house in a certain defined small area must put a basket of food outside the door on each day of the week. If no basket was there when the guerrillas came to collect, everyone in the household who should have provided it would be killed.

The early stages of the twelve-year campaign by Communist guerrillas in Malaya provided a glaring example of the use of terrorism in its 'propaganda of the deed' role: the use of terror in order to advertise the presence of a revolutionary movement and its ability to strike with ease and impunity. In one of many similar incidents a guerrilla platoon descended on a rubber plantation, seized four rubber-tappers, and then slit their throats one by one in front of their fellow workers. Noel Barber, author of *The War of the Running Dogs*, has commented: 'there seemed no reason for it—except the obvious one of striking terror into the hearts of simple people.'[8]

The rubber-tapping population was an important source of potential logistic support for the guerrillas, and if such support was not willingly forthcoming ruthless attempts were made to try and induce it. As well as any tappers themselves who failed to

[8] Noel Barber, *War of the Running Dogs*, Collins (London, 1971), p. 51

61

cooperate their families were equally likely to fall victim to terrorist methods of persuasion. A guerrilla detachment appeared in a village one night and ordered three tappers who had refused to pay subscriptions to the Communists to present their wives and children. One child from each family was then selected and cut to pieces in front of their parents, who were then told to 'pay up' or another of their children would be similarly treated.

One tapper who refused to collect subscriptions for the guerrillas was tied to a tree and his arms cut off one by one. Two local government councillors were kidnapped and a few days later their wives received a parcel containing one of each of their husband's arms, together with a note demanding food and stating that unless such food was supplied within a week the other arms would be sent.

In Malaya terrorism was also used in a systematic attempt to damage the country's economy by wrecking the rubber industry upon which it depended. This attempt took the form of a sustained campaign of assassination aimed at European plantation managers and their assistants, and large-scale slashing of rubber trees. The number of deaths through terrorism rose to a peak of 646 in 1950, and in the same year 106 people were also reported missing. At the end of 1951, however, the leaders of the guerrilla forces decided that terrorism had been used in too unselective a manner and had been counter-productive, alienating much of the population. They therefore gave orders that targets for attack should be chosen with greater care.

In Algeria terrorism was used by the Nationalist forces under the command of the FLN both as a weapon of psychological warfare against the French colonial population and in order to obtain support from the mass of the Muslim population. Against the French settlers it was used indiscriminately in order to cause demoralization and induce flight, and also to deliberately arouse hatred and distrust of the Muslim population with the aim of provoking unauthorized acts of retaliation by settlers against Muslims, and so in turn inflaming Muslim opinion against the settlers. In this last aim it succeeded only too well.

Against the Muslim population it was used in a more selective fashion but with equal success. In the early part of the revolt and indeed for much of its course the FLN found considerable difficulty in arousing the necessary degree of mass support to ensure success. In order to guarantee a less hesitant reception of its efforts a deliberate policy was embarked upon of liquidating known pro-French Muslims and those serving in official positions under the Government. Ultimately this policy was extended to include the assassination of French-appointed *caids*, or village headmen, and all unsympathetic opinion leaders, such as local government officials, school teachers, and doctors.

In the cities, assassinations were largely effected by special political cells, whilst bomb attacks on European-owned premises and indiscriminate attacks on crowds were carried out by military cells of the underground organization. The FLN were well aware of the propaganda value of terrorist attacks in large cities where foreign press men were likely to be present, and one FLN spokesman openly stated:

'Is it better for our cause to kill ten of our enemies in a remote village where this will not cause comment, or to kill only one man in Algiers where the American press will get hold of the story the next day ... if we are going to take risks, we must ensure that people learn about our struggle.'[9]

Although well-organized the FLN terrorist network in the cities was at first handicapped in its work by its members' lack of knowledge in handling explosives and bomb making. This limitation, plus a lack of essential equipment, forced its cells into contact with the more experienced Communist party, who somewhat reluctantly, and for fear of being outpaced, agreed to give technical aid. This help was hardly well repaid, for later the Nationalist FLN command was to ruthlessly destroy the power of the Communist party by allocating its squads to what it knew to be suicide missions, resulting in their decimation.

By the end of 1956 the FLN terrorists in Algiers had obtained almost complete control of the 80,000-strong Muslim population of the Casbah, although probably no more than 4,000 members of the population were involved in the terrorist network. Although this stranglehold was later to be broken for a time by General Massu and his paratroopers, FLN terrorism and Government concessions to it succeeded ultimately in producing the backlash from extremist settlers which had always been one of its aims.

[9] Jaques Duchemin, *Histoire Du FLN* (Paris, 1962), p. 263

63

The embodiment of this backlash, in the shape of the OAS and its campaign of indiscriminate counter-terrorism against the Muslim population and liberal Europeans, brought a chaotic turn to events and a serious threat to the stability of the French state itself.[10]

In Cyprus, Grivas's entire campaign was based on the use of terrorism as a psychological weapon. Realizing that it would be impossible to defeat the British Army in a normal guerrilla campaign, he calculated that a protracted period of selective killing and widespread intimidation would soon demoralize the local police and administration, and within a measurable period make the British Government and British public opinion anxious to wash its hands of the 'Cyprus problem'. 'Unfriendly' policemen were among the first targets for attack, and warnings were issued to Greek Cypriot policemen suggesting that they should resign from the Force, and saying, 'Do not try to block our path or you will stain it with your blood.'

Police morale was particularly badly shattered by the murder of a Special Branch detective in the middle of Nicosia in August; this incident, which seemed to show how easily policemen could be attacked and killed, even in the heart of the island's capital, resulted in a large number of resignations from the Police Force.

An operation order of Grivas's explained in precise terms the object of the campaign against the police:

> 'The aim of our next offensive will be to terrorize the police and to paralyse the administration, both in the towns and in the countryside ... Disillusionment will spread through the Police Force so rapidly that most of them, if they do not actually help us, will turn a blind eye to our activities.'[11]

A special example was made by arranging for the murder of members of the Police Force known for their keenness and efficiency in as public a place as possible, and a point was made of attacking police patrols in the countryside in order to dissuade the police from straying far from the towns.

[10] It is perhaps of interest that not a few members of the OAS were defectors from the Algerian Communist Party, which for many years had supported the union of Algeria and France for tactical reasons.

[11] Grivas, *The Memoirs of General Grivas*, Longmans, Green (London, 1964), p. 38

This steady undermining of the morale and effectiveness of the Police Force resulted in the authorities being increasingly unable to protect the population from intimidation, and fear of EOKA reprisals to anyone who in any way helped the Government quickly grew. Grivas was ruthless in dealing with real or suspected informers. He even planned to send a special execution squad to London to hunt down and kill Cypriots who had given information to the security forces and then fled the country. He believed that the shooting of 'even three or four Cypriots in London would create an enormous sensation' giving 'well worthwhile' results. The scheme which included plans for the formation of similar squads in Africa and Australia was, however, vetoed by Archbishop Makarios: much to the disappointment of Grivas, who considered that a splendid chance had been lost to 'show the strength of the organization on an international scale'.

EOKA methods of intimidation included the issuing of warnings, beatings-up, and shooting. The shooting of those who had angered EOKA was usually carried out in the circumstances of the greatest possible publicity in order to impress others. On one occasion two EOKA gunmen entered a Greek Orthodox Church whilst a service was in progress, lined up the congregation and shot dead a member of the choir who had been on EOKA's wanted list. Altogether 218 Greek Cypriots died as the result of EOKA action, as compared with eighty-four British servicemen.

A very important part in EOKA terrorist activities was carried out by the so-called 'town execution groups' which struck repeatedly at members of the security forces and others. Grivas has given a graphic account of the high level of activity and methods of these groups in referring to the 'execution group' in Nicosia commanded by 'a youth of dash and spirit':

'... a week later Sofocleus led a daylight attack on two soldiers in Ledra Street, which at the time, was full of shoppers looking for Christmas presents. One soldier was killed and the other wounded ... Next Sofocleus undertook the execution of a British agent called Savvas Porakos, who ran a Nicosia hotel; bursting into the private room where Porakos was dining with his son-in-law, a British Police Officer ... the group sprayed the room with machine-gun fire. Porakos was killed and Williams badly wounded ...

65

Twelve days later they chose as a target a British officer who, they had observed, walked every morning from his hotel to a taxi rank where he would take a cab to Army headquarters at Wolsey Barracks. Two of Sofocleus's group made the attack while a third kept watch. The officer, hit by five bullets at point-blank range, fell in the road, then got up and staggered a few paces before collapsing dead. The same group were responsible for the first attack on RAF members. This was carried out in the busy shopping centre around Ledra Street, in broad daylight. Sofocleus and his four fighters moved through the streets with sten guns concealed under their gabardine raincoats, passing a military patrol as they went: they then followed their target, three airmen, up the street, overtook them, turned and opened fire. Two died on the spot and the third staggered down the street with four bullet holes in his back and collapsed in a shop . . . Such was the work of the town execution groups.'[12]

Grivas has also made special mention of another typical incident of the work of such groups:

'At 6 p.m. they saw a Briton watering his garden with a hose. Pavlou walked up to the garden wall and shot him once at close range; then as he screamed and fell, fired three more shots into the body and escaped with his companion . . . they heard on the radio the next day that the man was a colonel. I sent my congratulations on this attack.'

EOKA's campaign of physical terrorism and intimidation was closely tied to other more indirect measures, such as the organization of an enforced boycott of local Cypriot papers which did not show 'the correct spirit' in supporting EOKA's demands or in voicing opposition to Government security measures. Falling sales often brought a more cooperative attitude on the part of editors.

Towards the end of the campaign a boycott of British goods was also organized under EOKA's direction, which in addition ordered the removal of all British lettering and signs from shops, streets and advertisements; pressure was brought for the dismissal of all British employees working for Cypriot firms.

[12] Grivas, *The Memoirs of General Grivas*, Longmans, Green (London, 1964), p. 38

In Aden, the terrorist campaign that resulted in British withdrawal in 1966 was almost wholly the tool of Egyptian policy, and the determination of the Government of President Nasser to rid the Arabian Peninsular and the Persian Gulf of British influence. The National Front For the Liberation of the Occupied South (Yemen) had a headquarters in Cairo, and issued almost daily military communiqués through its political secretary, which were given the greatest prominence in the Egyptian press and radio.

The National Liberation Front's main operational base was at Ta'z in the Yemen. Recruits to the organization were here given training in terrorist techniques under Egyptian instructors, equipped with arms and explosives usually originating in the Soviet bloc, and were then sent into the South Arabia Federation or the town of Aden to begin operations. The Front was organized in a cell system with various district commands. The Police Special Branch became a main target for attack and within a comparatively short time its original membership had been almost entirely liquidated by assassination or resignations enforced by intimidation. All Arabs working for the British administration were also prime targets, and acts of terrorism were supplemented by a stream of threats over Cairo Radio, which would quite often pick out personalities by name, against all who in any way assisted the British. As the campaign progressed the wives and children of British service men were also drawn on to the list of targets and frequent attacks were carried out in the 'Maala Mile' district of Aden where many British families lived. Attacks with hand grenades were often carried out in crowded streets causing heavy casualties amongst innocent Arab passers-by.

Training given to terrorists by the Egyptian intelligence service was extremely thorough and included counter-interrogation courses. In one case it was found that a terrorist brought in for questioning had been taught how to simulate a fainting fit, so as to avoid having to answer awkward questions.

As 1972 came to a close, it seemed possible that a new upsurge of guerrilla activity was about to take place. Reports spoke of a major guerrilla offensive against Portuguese Guinea possibly being imminent and there was a sudden increase in guerrilla activity in the Zambesi valley. With few exceptions the guerrilla groups active in Southern Africa are Marxist-orientated, relying almost exclusively on military supplies from the Soviet Bloc or Communist China, and dependent to a large degree on the same sources for the training of their cadres; although at the same time being in receipt of considerable propaganda and financial aid, in particular from some Scandinavian countries and certain international organizations.

Those groups considered to be the spearheads of the guerrilla campaign, those operating against Portuguese rule in Portuguese Guinea, Angola, and Mozambique have adopted sophisticated plans for the administration of 'liberated' territory and the attraction of support from amongst the local population. Amilcar Cabrai, secretary-general of PAIGC (African Party for the Independence of Guinea and the Cape Verdes) claimed, for instance, at a meeting in London in 1971:

'Since our Congress of Cassaca in 1964 we have maintained a clear distinction between the functions of the different instruments of the party. We distinguished between the role of the party, whose main task lies in political work, and the role of the armed forces, guerrilla or regular, whose task is to take action against the Portuguese colonialists. At the same time we created all the organs necessary for national reconstruction work in liberated areas.

'We have, therefore, no really great problems in moving from the structure of a guerrilla struggle to the structures of mass participation. We are organized as a party: by village, by zone and by region. Southern Guinea is led by a National Committee of Liberated Regions in the South, and the north is led by a National Committee of Liberated Regions in the North. This forms a basic structure of government. The liberated regions in fact already contain all the elements of a state—administrative services, health services, education services, local armed forces for defence against Portuguese attacks, tribunals and prisons. The immediate problem is to move from the liberated to the non-liberated areas, and to enlarge our state till it encloses the whole country. The transition to state structure will not be a problem.'[13]

[13] *Our People Are Our Mountains*, Committee for Freedom in Mozambique, Angola and Guinea, p. 16

68

Similar claims have been made by the leaders of FRELIMO (Frente de Libertaco de Moçambique) the guerrilla group operating in Mozambique. The available evidence, however, indicates that in fact none of the groups operating in Portuguese Africa have so far succeeded in establishing anything approaching control over more than a few scattered and in general extremely sparsely inhabited tracts of territory close to the frontiers of the country in which they operate. Without exception their main bases lie outside Portuguese territory and the extent to which they have been forced to use terrorist tactics against 'uncooperative' elements of the local population would seem to indicate that their propaganda has not yet made any deep appeal. They would, therefore, seem to have had little chance to put such elaborate plans as those outlined above into effective practice.

CHAPTER IV

Vietnam—Testing Ground for Revolution

The war-blasted and tortured country of Vietnam remains the prime testing ground for the practical application of theories of revolutionary People's War. The tactical fighting methods of the Viet Cong and the extremely efficient and complex paramilitary and political network of supporting organizations created by the National Liberation Front have become models for revolutionaries throughout the Third World, and will no doubt long remain so, whatever the outcome of the present struggle.

Whilst much has been written on the expertise of the Viet Cong in the arts of guerrilla warfare, less has appeared concerning their equally expert use of propaganda, psychological warfare and terrorism in order to ensure civilian support, all of which have been such a feature of this campaign.

It should be noted, however, that whilst the tactics and organizational techniques described were instrumental in enabling the Communist revolutionary forces to obtain a firm grip on large areas of the country up to and including the Tet offensive of 1968, a radical change in the situation had occurred by the end of 1970. For by that time patient and imaginative counter-insurgency work, which involved the use of political and psychological methods almost as much as military, and which was commenced by the South Vietnamese and allied forces in the wake of the failure of the Tet offensive, had bought substantial results in very largely loosening this grip. By the late summer of

1971, it was estimated, for instance, that over 95 per cent of the population of South Vietnam were living in areas which had been either completely pacified, freed, or partially freed of Communist control.

There would seem little doubt that it was the severe reverses suffered by the Viet Cong from 1968 onwards, from which there seemed little chance of it recovering, and the smashing of much of the supporting political infrastructure established with such care by the National Liberation Front, that led to the decision to commit the North Vietnamese Regular Army to a full-scale conventional invasion of the South in the spring of 1972 in an attempt to reverse the position.

The need for the South Vietnamese Army to concentrate almost its entire strength upon combating this invasion, together with the disappearance of allied ground forces from the battlefield, offered obvious new opportunities for the Viet Cong and its political arm to re-establish themselves in some of the areas from which they had been almost eliminated.

THE ORGANIZATIONAL WEAPON

The mainspring of the Viet Cong effort to obtain psychological control of the population of South Vietnam has consisted of a vast machine engaged in spinning a country-wide web of committees, fronts, and cells of almost every conceivable description. Its aim is to enmesh all categories of the population in active support for the revolutionary cause in areas under the control of the Communist forces; and, in areas outside their control or still disputed, to destroy support for the Government's forces amongst the civilian population, and to bring about a collapse of military morale.

The direction of this mammoth effort is primarily in the hands of the People's Revolutionary Party, in fact the southern branch of the ruling Communist Labour Party of North Vietnam. The leaders of the People's Revolutionary Party (PRP) receive general directives from the supreme command of the insurrection, Hanoi's Central Office for South Vietnam (COSVN). The PRP is assisted in its efforts by a number of front and other organizations, chief of which is the National Liberation Front, a nominally separate body over which in practice the party has complete control.

Directed by a Central Committee, the NLF operates through a series of provincial and district committees; at village level it is usually most actively represented in Communist-controlled areas by specialized bodies, such as Farmers' Liberation Associations, Youth Liberation Associations, Cultural Liberation Associations, Women's Liberation Associations, Student Liberation Associations, or the Workers' Liberation Associations, which operate chiefly in rubber-growing areas.

Altogether there are about twenty different organizations under the NLF's management, including two political parties—the Radical Socialist Party and a similar front organization. There are in addition a number of 'special interest groups' such as Veterans' Organizations and the Patriotic and Democratic Journalists' Association. In 1969 it was estimated that about 40,000 full-time cadres were employed in the service of the NLF and its component organizations, and that altogether it could probably claim the allegiance of about 750,000 people.

Douglas Pike has written that one of the main characteristics of the NLF is the 'blurring of the line between the political and the military between war and peace', and has said that:

'. . . The NLF is in tune with the nihilism of the second half of the twentieth century, the spirit of rebellion for its own sake, the blanket condemnation of all establishments, the drive to harness the alienated, and the injection of violence into the forefront of political change regardless of cost.'[1]

The People's Revolutionary Party has since 1966 maintained its own parallel structure to that of the NLF in occupied areas. In the more recent years of the campaign, and particularly after the failure of the Tet offensive of 1968, increasing emphasis has been put on the formation of People's Liberation Committees. These committees have the task of governing the life of villages and hamlets in Viet Cong-occupied areas under the direction of the party. Farmers' Youth and Women's Liberation Associations are the base upon which these committees are built, and

[1] Douglas Pike, *War, Peace and the Viet Cong*, The M.I.T. Press, Massachusetts Institute of Technology (Massachusetts, 1969), p. 9

members of each committee are elected. But the party carefully screens all candidates, and one of the qualifications for election is to have taken part in combat against Government forces.

Party control over its military wing, the Viet Cong guerrillas, is, in the words of a party directive, 'absolute, direct and complete'. At the highest level this control is vested in a Central Military Affairs Committee at Party Headquarters. Directly responsible to this committee is the Viet Cong's Political Affairs Department, which in turn supervises the working of regional military affairs committees and the political commissars and political officers attached to each guerrilla unit. Command of Viet Cong units is shared between the military commander and the political commissar, who are both allotted equal responsibility.

In the months immediately before the opening of the Tet Offensive in February 1968, a whole host of new Communist-controlled organizations made their appearance, whose role was to conduct propaganda campaigns and incite unrest in Government areas, so as to prepare the ground for the 'general uprising' to which it was hoped the offensive would lead. These organizations took many forms: 'peace-loving Buddhist soldiers', 'revolutionary council', 'uprising committees', et cetera. After the failure of the offensive a number of these new organizations that survived were banded together into a new federation, known as the Alliance of National and Democratic Peace Forces of South Vietnam.

In Government-controlled areas the NLF's clandestine organization is largely based upon a cell system, as is general with communist organizations, a three-man cell being the type most favoured. These cells are allotted particular tasks which may be of a political, propaganda or terrorist nature. A particularly sophisticated cell system is used as a base for operations in towns and cities, the most complex being in the capital, Saigon. Here as in other cities two or three cells sometimes join together to form special operating teams. Activities of cells include tax collecting, propaganda and political indoctrination, party committee cells dealing with such subjects as civil affairs and youth groups, and coordinating cells that move backwards and forwards from central areas of the city to the suburbs. There are also a number of special penetration cells, cells performing reconnaissance functions, and the terrorist cells. The latter are chiefly comprised of the so-called 'special activity' cells which specialize in assassination, and the sapper cells specializing in sabotage and the use of explosives.

THE NLF PLAN OF SUBVERSION

The NLF strategy throughout the greater part of the campaigns has been devoted to preparing for a *khoi Nghia*, or general uprising, of the people of South Vietnam against their Government. These preparations are aimed at destroying the will of the Government and its followers to resist the revolution by a protracted period of intensive terrorism, propaganda, and political warfare. In early 1968 the NLF judged that these preparations had been so far advanced that the time for the launching of the general uprising was indeed ripe. But its judgement was proved faulty and its policies became once again based upon the idea of protracted struggle with the day of *khoi Nghia* as a somewhat remote target.

The preparatory operations are embraced in what is known as *Dau Tranh*, or the 'struggle movement'. The overwhelming importance of the struggle movement in the thinking of NLF cadre members has been explained by one defector from their ranks. *Dau Tranh*, he has said, influences all their thinking, behaviour, attitudes, work, every aspect of their lives. Their very existence is dominated by it.

The *Dau Tranh* programme is divided into three sections: *Dan Van, Dich Van,* and *Binh Van.*

Dan Van consists of action amongst the people in Communist-controlled areas, and is aimed at consolidating the Communist hold upon them, recruiting their support for the revolutionary cause, creating safe base areas from which the Viet Cong can operate, and presenting a propaganda picture of the perfection of life in 'liberated areas'.

Dich Van concerns action aimed at the civilian population in Government-controlled areas, a thoroughgoing propaganda and psychological warfare campaign carried on by armed propaganda teams and all other available media. Propaganda to influence foreign public opinion is also included under this section.

Binh Van consists of propaganda action amongst South Viet-

74

namese armed service personnel, and amongst civilians in the employ of the Government. Its primary object is to decisively lower the morale of those against whom it is employed, and its long-term object is to produce large-scale defection. To attain these an intensive war is pursued of nerves, intimidation, and undercover agents to penetrate the Civil service and fighting services.

The importance of this campaign of political warfare in the eyes of the Revolutionary High Command, as compared with the purely military effort of the Viet Cong, can be seen from the fact that it has been estimated that during the years 1959 to 1963 90 per cent of all trained cadres were assigned to duties under the *Van* programme. Despite an upswing to the military side between 1966 and 1968 the percentage of cadres engaged upon *Van* work never, it is thought, fell below 60 per cent of the total available and by 1971 had increased again to 70 per cent.

POLITICAL WARFARE TACTICS

One of the main instruments upon which the NLF and the Viet Cong place the greatest reliance for obtaining the practical support of the population of areas under their control are the Farmers' Liberation Associations. In addition to imparting a sound political education, these associations are supposed to rapidly draw the entire peasant population of the area into the service of the revolution. They are, for instance, supposed to oversee the implementation of a quota system for collecting rice for use as guerrilla fighters' rations, and to the same end to encourage each family to grow food surplus to their requirements. One captured association instruction advocated that vegetables should be grown 'even on breastworks or bomb craters'.

Each farming family is encouraged to store grain and salt in their homes as a reserve for use by Viet Cong forces who may be forced to take refuge in the village in an emergency. The associations are also expected to see that every farmer provides himself with some sort of homemade weapon with which to fight the Government forces, should they come; and to see that every farmer over the age of sixteen contributes to the village defences by building a stake pit. The women of the village are whenever possible persuaded to take over most of the work on the land,

75

and to encourage their husbands or sons to join the guerrillas.

Suggested activities for one Farmers' Association in Quang Nam Province included the calling of a conference for 'aged men' at which it was intended to induce the assembled elders to persuade their sons and grandsons to join the Viet Cong. It was hoped that as a result of the indoctrination they received, the old men would also themselves 'assume production work in the rear in support of the revolution'.

Yet another function of the Farmers' Associations is the organization of teams of porters from the peasant population for the transportation of supplies for the Viet Cong, a vital factor in the latter's logistic system: 'On the basis of each person's health, determine the quantity of rice to be transported by each person,'[2] said a passage in the instructions quoted from above.

The revolutionary war effort also receives much practical aid from the Women's Liberation Associations. These have the task of recruiting women and girls not only for non-combatant tasks but also for front-line duties. During the preparations for the Tet Offensive, for instance, at the end of 1967, Women's Associations were called upon to engage in a recruiting campaign to raise the number of female guerrilla fighters in some Viet Cong units to as much as 50 per cent of their total strength. At the same time they were ordered to oversee the establishment of one permanent platoon of women labourers in each village under Communist control, to handle food supplies, care for and transport the wounded, and take part in general liaison work. Each village Women's Association was also supposed to establish a special cell for the collection of funds in support of the revolution.

Members of the Women's Associations are also entrusted with welfare work amongst the dependents of men fighting with the Viet Cong. In addition they are often given important tasks in areas outside Communist control. For example, during these same preparations Women's Liberation Associations were instructed to 'propagandize, educate, mobilize, and organize' the women in the cities and government-controlled provinces. They were advised to build cells of between three and five women in

[2] *Documents and Research Notes*, United States Mission to Vietnam (Saigon)

such areas and to organize 'propaganda assault teams' which would disseminate propaganda in the market places of the country's main towns. Association members were also bidden to 'strive to subvert enemy soldiers and officers'.

The Youth Liberation Associations perform an equally important role. Their main function would seem to be to recruit youths and even children as young as eleven or ten for both combatant and other tasks. Boys in their teens or younger are not infrequently used to perform terrorist attacks, and efforts have often been made by the Youth Associations to recruit them into the so-called 'determined-to-die' squads; small expendable groups used for well-publicized suicide missions. Recruits for these squads are frequently put through special initiation ceremonies in which public bathing and tea-drinking play an important part.

The recruiting role of the Youth Associations has become all the more important owing to the extremely heavy casualties suffered by the Viet Cong during and after the Tet Offensive, and the need to find replacements. In some cases associations have been ordered to assist in the drafting of all males aged from nine to fifteen in their areas into local guerrilla units. Defectors have spoken of boys of eleven taking part in combat, whilst one expert in Saigon has claimed that the ranks of the Viet Cong have been so decimated that the majority of rank-and-file members of the force are now aged between fourteen and seventeen.

In January 1970, intelligence sources in Saigon announced that they had information that the National Liberation Front had launched a nation-wide drive to recruit children from South Vietnam for long periods of training in the Communist-ruled North. The idea apparently was that when these children had been fully trained they would be sent back into the south as guerrillas, spies, terrorists, or political cadres. The scheme was believed to have been initiated about three years earlier. In theory, children sent to the North were supposed to be aged between ten and seventeen, but it was thought that in practice considerable numbers below the age of ten had been sent. Children selected for training were often orphans or relatives of Viet Cong cadres; their recruiters were said to go to considerable trouble to make them feel that a great honour had been done them by their selection. Once arrived in North Vietnam the older children received comparatively short periods of training, but those of a younger age were embarked upon courses of instruction intended to last several years.

The People's Revolutionary Councils, together with NLF and Party cadres, have the job of overseeing every aspect of the lives of the people who live in the villages under their control. Considerable emphasis is placed upon 'cultural tasks', usually the responsibility of a special cultural and information section, which normally mean the institution of a boycott of Government broadcasts, Government newspapers and propaganda literature and other 'enemy' reading material. The people are encouraged to search out and destroy examples of the 'servile art and culture of the enemy' and to reject 'reactionary entertainment', 'sex-appeal images' and such, as well as being enjoined to: '... Conduct progressive activities to make the rural area display a new face under the people's revolutionary administration...'; and to 'Improve and perfect the cultural and information machinery in villages and hamlets, which includes the cultural and information section, hamlet cultural and information sub-section and other work teams, namely loudspeaker teams, propaganda assault teams, entertainment cells etc., ... so that it will be capable of undertaking ideological indoctrination, politically motivating the people to achieve victory, meeting the people's spiritual needs in arts and culture...'[3]

Other Revolutionary Council sections or committees look after public health and education, and attempt to provide one school giving courses of highly politically motivated education not only in each village, but even in each hamlet.

The general direction of propaganda activities is usually in the hands of People's Revolutionary Party Propaganda and Indoctrination section. The chief of this at Provincial Party Headquarters is responsible for running training courses for all propaganda and indoctrination cadres in his province. His head-quarters section is also responsible for printing posters and leaflets, and for distributing political books and magazines.

[3] *Documents and Research Notes*, United States Mission to Vietnam (Saigon)

Village Propaganda and Indoctrination section leaders must be good speakers, and often take part themselves in the routine work of conducting indoctrination sessions for villagers. One important duty is that of writing reports on Party members for forwarding to District Headquarters, on the development of the party's work and on the results obtained by each propaganda campaign. They direct their cadres in the use of a much-favoured propaganda weapon—the megaphone, and also in copious slogan-writing on walls. They are supposed to spend considerable time on sponsoring the formation of the various Liberation Associations, and on persuading the local population of the benefits of staying in or returning to 'liberated' villages. They choose teachers for the schools and select books for the syllabus.

Propaganda work in the field is divided into two main categories, that focused on the civilian population, and that focused on the Armed Forces and Government officials. These two categories of work are each carried out under the supervision of separate directing staffs, with their own section chiefs at each level of command. The chiefs of the civilian propaganda sections are in effect the chief recruiting officers for all Communist-controlled organizations, both military and political. Not infrequently they personally direct activities of the Farmers' Youth and Women's Liberation Associations. Highly trained cadre party members, they and their sections are key elements in the drive to obtain popular support for the National Liberation Front, and to enrol the inhabitants of every village it controls in mass organizations supporting its policies.

When a major offensive is under way it is the task of the chiefs of civilian propagandizing teams to do their utmost to rally the people to take part in a mass uprising against the Government. Normally they and their subordinates are most active in contested areas.

The main function of the military propagandizing sections is to induce Government and allied troops to defect. A favourite tactic used by members of these sections is to contact members of the families of men serving in the Government forces and persuade them to influence their sons or husbands to desert. Their secondary role is to plant agents in the ranks of Government forces and civil servants.

Captured orders of one military propagandizing section read:
'We must work out a specific plan for propagandizing
and motivating puppet troops at each post and unit. We
must plant agents in these places to conduct political
indoctrination ... We must try to restrict all enemy activities
and recruit more agents in enemy units ... In areas where
there are American and satellite troops, we must make them
read our leaflets and slogans to stimulate their opposition to
military operations, as well as their desire to go home.'[4]

An extremely sophisticated system of underground work has
been established in order to enable the party and NLF organizations to operate in contested areas; and even to some extent in
areas under Government control. Senior Party officials and cadres
in such areas have probably three or more houses in which they
can sleep on successive nights, each of these houses having a hiding place in or near them in which refuge can be taken. The most
senior party officials such as Province and District Party secretaries seldom move outside safe base areas. In contested and other
dangerous areas most activity is carried on only at night, and
then never for more than a comparatively short time in any one
place. Village party secretaries of the PRP may live in the woods
outside their village, returning only during the hours of darkness
to direct operations.

Where members of village party organizations and supporting
organizations have been arrested nocturnal visits are sometimes
paid to the village by cadres from district headquarters, escorted
by guerrillas, with the object of collecting taxes, warning the
villagers against cooperating with the government, and 're-
educating' the families of Government soldiers.

The underground system has been developed to the highest
pitch of efficiency in the cities, where the revolutionary cadres
have to operate in an environment wholly controlled by the
Government. Usually committee meetings of city branches of the
People's Revolutionary Party are held in some safe hamlet or
other secure location just outside the city. In the city itself, cells
and sections meet at pre-arranged times in busy places such as
snack bars, soup shops, and doctors' surgeries, members travelling

[4] *Documents and Research Notes*, United States Mission to Vietnam
(Saigon)

to and from the meeting place in the early morning or evening rush hour to prevent suspicion. Often a cell leader will wait in the meeting place for cell members to approach him one after the other to receive orders or pass on information.

The Tet Offensive was preceded by a large-scale propaganda campaign in which the underground network in the cities played a great part. One young man later described to the police how he and his eighteen-year-old sister were recruited, in January 1968, by underground agents in Saigon to act as leaflet distributors. He was told that if he undertook this work he would later be made an 'armed propaganda agent', and that when Saigon had been occupied he would be promoted to the post of a 'Viet Cong Security Agent'.

After his second leaflet-distributing mission he was given a pistol, instructed in its use and told to shoot rather than be arrested. When the Tet Offensive actually broke out he was assigned as bodyguard to an important propaganda cadre, whose primary function was to address crowds through a megaphone in order to obtain their support.

The importance given to propaganda and political work during this major Communist onslaught can be seen from the fact that it has been estimated that for every five guerrilla fighters in action, at least one propaganda or political cadre was at work. Great stress was placed in preparatory instructions on the need to obtain the support of all the people and the spreading of disruption by such tactics as the incitement of strikes.

Viet Cong units were themselves drawn into the propaganda battle with these instructions:

> 'Everyone from the commanding officer on down to individual soldier must, throughout the period of uprising, have in his possession such items as drums and gongs and sabotage equipment. Must engage in propaganda action targeted at the population at large. Must regiment the masses.'[5]

During attacks by Viet Cong units on targets in cities in the early days of the offensive it was common to find propaganda cadres encircling the area where action was taking place,

[5] *Documents and Research Notes*, United States Mission to Vietnam (Saigon)

explaining to the anxious crowds what was happening and appealing for support.

The vast quantities of propaganda literature produced by the revolutionary propaganda machine is illustrated from figures quoted in a report by just one Provincial Military Propagandizing section in December 1967. It stated that in the previous nine months it had distributed 20,000 leaflets in South Korean, 7,000 leaflets in English, 2,500 leaflets in Vietnamese and 14,000 leaflets on the need to stimulate food production in support of the revolution.

An interesting feature of this report was the emphasis placed in notes on what was called 'Stimulating an anti-war movement and a movement to ask for repatriation'. It was explained that:

> 'This movement shall strike at the morale of the U.S. troops and their allies who are frightened by death and have a great dislike for this war. Through use of this method we must create a broad and intensive anti-war movement to ask for quick repatriation.'[6]

Under another heading, 'Launching the enemy against the enemy', it was noted that difficulties were often apparent in communications between American and South Vietnamese troops, and also in the relations between officers and soldiers. The exploitation of such difficulties in order to create discord and the self-destruction of enemy forces was strongly advocated, with the comment, 'This has been very effective in many places in the past.'

Importance has always been placed upon propaganda amongst members of religious groups, and was underlined by the issue of an NLF directive of early 1969 which called for the establishment of a regular system of propaganda work among members of the various religions and churches as a routine task. The directive ordered the formation of special sub-sections to take charge of this campaign, which should draw upon members from organizations already engaged in work among the peasants, youth and women, and upon those engaged in security duties.

The prime function of the sub-sections was defined as to guide

[6] *Documents and Research Notes*, United States Mission to Vietnam (Saigon)

other organizations in disseminating propaganda directed at religious communities and in particular to 'positively get a firm hold of the Catholic population'. They were also intended to collect detailed information, such as the number of religious believers in each village, the ideological leanings of religious leaders and their political activities, the activities of religious organizations, and the political beliefs of members of the various religions. Much play was to be made with the alleged freedom of worship under Communist rule; to attract recruits from amongst the religious-minded; and the campaign was to be extended to the towns and cities. A network of agents should be established in religious organizations:

> 'These networks will help gain the sympathy of the followers of the upper class and encourage the Buddhist and Catholic population to unite and rise up against the U.S., overthrow the puppet Government and seize power for the people ... We must properly apply the stratagem of the Party, which consists in winning over religious personnel, dividing and isolating them, and using different treatment for different people.'[7]

There has been some evidence that Communist agents have on occasion deliberately engineered clashes between different religious groups in order to create confusion amongst Government supporters and to heighten tension. One correspondent has related an instance of a South Vietnamese army jeep being stolen from a compound in Saigon. Not long afterwards the jeep was seen being driven slowly past the main Buddhist Headquarters by two men in army uniform, with a loudspeaker blaring the news that Catholic youths from a nearby suburb were going to burn down the Buddhist compound that night. Shortly afterwards the same jeep was seen outside a refugee settlement area, most of whose inmates were Roman Catholic. Here the message passed over its loudspeaker was that Buddhist gangs were planning to attack the settlement that same night; and would destroy its church.

As far as the police and intelligence authorities were aware

[7] *Documents and Research Notes*, United States Mission to Vietnam (Saigon)

neither community had had any intention of attacking each other at that time, but after the jeep had done its work both began to mobilize for action and a bloody riot was only barely averted. Later the jeep was found abandoned in an alley with not a sign of its two-man crew; there seemed every indication they had been Viet Cong agents.

Infiltration has always played a big part in the NLF's tactics of political warfare, but recently it has been given stronger emphasis. The particular targets for infiltration are professional groups, social organizations, friendship associations and student groups; Communist sympathizers are told to make every attempt to gain places on their executive committees. Considerable care and planning goes into infiltration attempts. An agent may join an organization and then carry out a careful study of the members who for any reason he thinks may be sympathetic to the cause. This period of study will probably last several months. When it is completed, the agent will form those he has selected into a 'fraction', who will then work under his direction to turn the organization into an anti-Government one.

The decrease of Viet Cong military activity and the possibilities of a negotiated peace led to an even greater stepping-up of the political warfare campaign on the part of the NLF and its component bodies. Cadres operating in Government-controlled and disputed areas were told to carry out propaganda amongst people of all walks of life. Renewed attempts were made to get members of Government soldiers' families to distribute anti-war propaganda literature amongst servicemen. Instructions were given to agents to obtain the sympathy of the war-wounded, widows and orphans, and to hold 'animated discussions with them' aimed at inciting them to 'demand the right to live'. American servicemen, including technicians and advisers attached to South Vietnamese units, became selected targets of the propaganda offensive. Propaganda Cadres were specially instructed to 'use slogans supporting and encouraging U.S. anti-war units and individuals to boost the struggles of U.S. servicemen'.

Instructions have also been issued on how use can be made of legal organizations, especially those to which many members of Government forces belong. Infiltrating agents will:

'Engage in discussions on our peace solution, and expose

the bellicosity of the Thieu-Ky-Kheim clique. Create a seething atmosphere, cleverly transform the discussions into hot debates leading the participants to come to blows. Disobey military operation orders, and oppose the special pacification operations.'[8]

At the same time they must concentrate on getting the population to listen to the broadcasts of the NLF's Liberation Radio.

TERRORISM

The use of cold and calculated terrorism by the Communist military and political forces in South Vietnam has gone hand in hand with the use of propaganda and psychological warfare, and has even been, as is often the case, an integral part of the latter. In terms of loss of life and human suffering it has wrought results far surpassing those in any other post-war insurrectionary campaign.

Terrorism was an integral part of the tactics used by the Viet Minh as early as the closing days of the Second World War. The Viet Minh forces under Vo Nguyen Giap embarked upon a policy of systematically exterminating all prominent non-Communist members of the nationalist movement whom they could reach. During the war against the French, vigorous attempts were made to eliminate all who had in any way caused themselves to be regarded as enemies of the resistance.

Terrorism first began to emerge as a serious threat to the stability of the newly-born state of South Vietnam about 1960. As that year opened, the number of murders by Viet Cong terrorists was averaging one a day. A rapid rise in the rate of assassination then took place, and in the two years culminating in the end of 1961 no less than 6,130 civilians had been murdered and 6,213 abducted (excluding battle casualties).

The main targets for terrorist attack in the early days of the war were local Government officials, teachers, medical workers, village headmen and everybody who might offer leadership to the local population in opposing the revolution. As the years passed and the power of the Viet Cong grew, this policy was pursued with ever greater thoroughness, until it came in many

[8] *Documents and Research Notes*, United States Mission to Vietnam (Saigon)

85

areas of the country to represent the almost complete genocide of the most educated and responsible elements in the community. During one year, 1964, 436 village headmen and other minor local officials were murdered, and over 1,300 kidnapped. By the end of 1965 the total number of civilians murdered or kidnapped as a result of terrorist action had grown to at least 25,000. At this time an average of 135 local officials were being murdered or kidnapped each month.

Complete records of deaths of civilians other than officials through terrorist action were not kept until the spring of 1967, but it has been estimated that, for each official, probably four ordinary civilians died. The group that has suffered particularly throughout the campaign has been the civilian workers of the Government's revolutionary development programme, subsequently named the Pacification Programme. Their task is to restore normal life to areas hard-hit by the fighting and to raise the standard of living in the most undeveloped areas of the country.

As the Viet Cong found both military success and voluntary support from the population harder to obtain, so has the scope of terrorism been extended. One expert has written:

'It is violence against the individual villager in his own village—assassination, execution or kidnapping that strikes home hardest. Turgid accounts of the "struggle movement" led by the Viet Cong or endless claims of military victories by agitprop teams mean little to the peasant. But when death strikes in his village, against someone he knows, a scar of fear is formed in his mind.'[9]

Sometimes in order to give some sort of legality to the process of summary execution victims have been condemned to death in their absence by 'people's courts', and informed of the sentence by letter or hand-delivered note. A Viet Cong cadre explained to Australian correspondent Wilfred Burchet the systematic way in which the movement has used the weapon of terrorism in attempts to extend its influence in the countryside:

'In each village we compiled a detailed dossier of the various local despots. If someone merited the death penalty

[9] *Viet Cong and the Use of Terrorism*, United States Mission to Vietnam (Saigon, 1967), p. 45

we sent a group to deal with him. Afterwards we used loud-hailers to explain the crimes committed . . . we posted names of other tyrants who would be dealt with if they did not cease their activities . . . the executions and the warnings played a major role in breaking the grip of the enemy throughout the country . . . and created conditions under which we could move back into the villages, either permanently or on organizational visits.'[9]

Viet Cong documents have listed fifteen different categories of persons as being fit subjects for terrorist action. These include: members of the police, intelligence and security services, special forces and psychological warfare units; members of what are termed 'reactionary political parties and organizations', Government officials of all types, key members of uncooperative social organizations such as women's and youth organizations and farmers' cooperatives; similar figures in cultural, art, press or propaganda bodies; leading members of religious organizations who are 'still deeply superstitious'; members of 'the exploiter class and their spouses who have not specifically sided with the workers', 'individuals with backward political tendencies', and 'relatives of persons engaged in working for intelligence or psychological warfare organizations'.

Attacks with explosives on Government offices, military establishments, business premises and places of entertainment have taken place periodically in Saigon and other cities. The main purpose of these attacks seemed to be to advertise the revolutionaries' power and to give an impression of their ability to strike anywhere at will, even in the most closely guarded areas. Although often prepared with the minutest attention to detail on the technical side, these attacks have most frequently been conducted without any thought as to the loss of innocent lives. In one case an attempt to blow up an American Army billet next door to a Saigon school was frustrated when the police arrested the terrorist who was to have placed the 260lb. bomb in the building. Told by the police that had the operation been successful and the bomb had exploded probably at least a hundred Vietnamese children would have been killed or injured, and asked whether he would not have felt remorse if this had happened, he replied: 'No, I wouldn't feel any remorse at all. This we cannot help.'

On other occasions when bombs have been placed in crowded places such as restaurants, there seems to have been a deliberate intention to kill as many civilians as possible, in order to create both a feeling of panic and resentment at the Government's and security forces' inability to prevent such things happening.

One terrorist tactic frequently used has been the use of inter-mittent harassing-fire at night against villages and hamlets. Such tactics, not infrequently accompanied by the shouting of propa-ganda slogans and taunts through megaphones, have sometimes been directed for weeks on end at particular villages. The object is to create the effect of an exhausting war of nerves, and at the same time to seek to prove that the Government is incapable of providing its followers with adequate protection.

American servicemen in recent years have been fairly low down the list of priorities for terrorist attack. The reason was explained in a Viet Cong document of 6 February 1967, which read in part:

'For a long time in Saigon, we concentrated on attacking Americans while overlooking the police and security agents (the latter are tracking down our agents) and the reactionary ringleaders (reactionary parties, disguised religious groups, spies, etc. . . .) who carry on their activities unpunished. If we destroy the Americans, they are capable of bringing in replacements; but if we succeed in destroying the suppressive government machinery, pacification apparatus, local tyrants, and reactionary ringleaders, we will have accomplished splendid achievements in favour of the revolution.'[10]

The terrorist side of the Viet Cong campaign is carried out in the main by three special types of paramilitary organization: special activity cells, sapper cells, and the South Vietnamese People's Liberation Security Forces.

Special activity cells operate both in the countryside and in the cities. Usually each is allocated a permanent area in which to work, and their speciality is assassination. Their principal weapon is the Soviet-made AK-47 submachine gun which has a folding

[10] *Viet Cong and the Use of Terrorism*, United States Mission to Vietnam (Saigon, 1967), p. 45

stock. These cells consist of highly trained and dedicated party members, but sometimes they may hire criminal elements or make use of local volunteers to assist them.

The sapper cells consist of specially trained members of the Viet Cong's military engineering forces. They operate mainly in urban areas, and have charge of all operations involving the use of explosives. They constitute an élite force, most of their members being North Vietnamese who have passed certain ideological examinations. Recruits have to be party members and must be nominated and seconded in their applications to join the force by other party members. Each cell has four members, and cells are then combined into detachments of between four and seven cells. Five such detachments constitute a sapper battalion, five battalions comprising a regiment.

Detachments normally specialize in some particular form of activity, for example reconnaissance work, transportation of explosives, or the manufacture or placing of charges.

The third main element in the Communist use of terrorism in Vietnam is the South Vietnamese People's Liberation Security Forces. In addition to being one of the main instruments for enforcing Communist rule in occupied areas, this force has the specified task of 'annihilating' any 'puppet ringleaders', members of 'reactionary political factions', and members of Government security and intelligence services.

It plays a major part in the Viet Cong punishment system in operation in areas under its control, which is aimed at eliminating all 'recalcitrant and reactionary elements who are actively opposing the revolution'. The punishments meted out to these elements are execution, sentences of imprisonment for periods up to twenty years, 'thought reform' and house arrest.

Those persons sentenced to 'thought reform' are liable to further punishment if their political attitudes do not change, being taken before a special court for re-sentencing if they continue to oppose the revolution.

The terrorist campaign is also aided by operations of 'paramilitary cells' who operate in some country areas, taking their orders from Provincial Party Headquarters, and making uncooperative political elements in less well-defended villages and hamlets their particular target.

Viet Cong members taking part in terrorist activity normally receive a special two-month course of training known as 'armed security training'; about 40 per cent of which consists of political indoctrination. Many acts of terrorism, however, particularly in the towns and cities, have been carried out by youths and sometimes even children locally recruited.

Sometimes these young terrorists are forced into action by threats to the safety of relatives or by direct physical coercion. In one far from isolated instance twenty-six people were killed and ninety-nine wounded when four grenades were thrown into a crowd in a hamlet in Dinh Tuong Province. It was discovered that the grenades had been thrown by four boys, three of them thirteen and one eleven, who were later arrested. It appeared that some weeks before the grenade incident they had been approached by a Viet Cong squad near the hamlet. The Viet Cong had threatened to kill them by holding their heads under water unless they did what was required of them. Terrified, they agreed, and were sent home with the grenades with instructions not to use them until they received orders to do so. They were told that if they informed the police of the plan they would be killed. Orders to carry out the attack on the crowd were later conveyed to them by a courier.

As well as using such methods of intimidation, however, Viet Cong terrorists have well exploited children's love of adventure and the excitement of having real toys, such as guns, in order to get their aid. One child psychologist who had interviewed a number of young Viet Cong defectors, amongst whom was one twelve-year-old boy who was reputed to have killed six policemen and one American soldier during the Tet Offensive, said: 'Most of the boys who go off with the V.C. are very naïve. They go for adventure and the promise of having their own guns. They are non-political.'[11]

A director of a centre for Viet Cong defectors explained further that:

'the V.C. knows what to promise these boys; the V.C. are masters of psychology, they know what a city boy is like, and

[11] *The Viet Cong and Children,* United States Mission to Vietnam (Saigon), p. 16

The front page of the Police News *of 17 September 1898, carrying the story of the Empress of Austria's assassination at the hands of the anarchist Luccheni*

RLES PEACE
AND
ALO BILL.

CK NUMBERS
STOCK.

THE ILLUSTRATED

POLICE NEWS

LAW COURTS.
AND WEEKLY RECORD
ESTABLISHED 1864

5. [REGISTERED FOR CIRCULATION IN THE UNITED KINGDOM AND ABROAD.]   SATURDAY, SEPT. 17, 1898.   Price One Penny.

SASSINATION OF THE EMPRESS OF AUSTRIA.

The storming of the Winter Palace in St Petersburg during the Russian Revolution

Lenin harangues the crowd in Petrograd, while Trotsky stands beside the platform (right)

Cyclists line up to salute Mussolini during the Fascist celebrations of November 1923

In Cyprus, 1956, an EOKA terrorist starts down a street in Nicosia

In 1967, a Nation
Liberation Front sniper s
his sights on the sm
township of Bir Ahm
fifteen miles from Ader

Yassir Arafat, guerri
leader of the Palest
Liberation Organization,
a 'front line area' in Jord

El Fatah guerrillas training in Jordan

A North Vietnamese propaganda photograph intended to show South Vietnamese Government or American troops (helmets were never worn by the Vietcong) taking peasants to put them in concentration camps. The actual people in the photograph are all members of Communist Cultural-Drama teams operating in the province of Kien Hoa

Members of the Provisional IRA

Tariq Ali lends his support to Krivine, the French Trotskyist leader, at a meeting in London in 1969

The 31st floor of the GPO Tower after the Angry Brigade's bomb had exploded there in October 1971

The scene at Lod Airport, Tel Aviv, in June 1972 after Japanese Red Army terrorists had killed 26 people and injured 70

On 5 September 1972, in the Olympic Village at Munich, an official of the Games negotiates with the leader of the Black September terrorists

what a country boy is like. A city boy may be promised a luxurious car to drive in and a big building to live in after the Communist liberation. A country boy may be promised his own gun and the chance to be taught Tai boxing.'[12]

One of the most chilling aspects of Viet Cong terrorism has been the use of a quota system prescribing the number of 'Government puppets', 'reactionary elements', and such, to be assassinated, 're-educated', or otherwise dealt with by district commands within certain periods. One such order from a province party committee stated that cells in each city ward or housing area must kill from two to five 'low-ranking tyrants' and one to two 'upper-level ring leaders'.

A report by the United States Mission in Vietnam on the use of terrorism by the Viet Cong says that Viet Cong cadres have found that terror 'turned on and off' somewhat surprisingly produces both pro- and anti-guerrilla feelings among villagers. Whilst at first its use breeds fear and hatred, with the first normally predominating, when it is 'turned off' for the time being after a period of intensive use in one area an exaggerated feeling of relief quickly spreads through the population, who tend to begin to regard the guerrillas as not nearly so inhumane as they in fact can be.

A major aim of Viet Cong terrorism has always been to dissuade the local population in country areas from making use of any social services provided by the Government, and to disrupt these services as much as possible. This policy has sometimes been carried to almost unimaginable extremes, as a report written by the American adviser to the South Vietnamese Army's IV Corps in 1969 demonstrates:

'They [the Communists] are particularly interested in closing schools in this area. For example, last month an armed propaganda team stopped a local school bus on a side road one morning and told the driver the children were not to attend school any more. The driver conveyed this message to the parents who could not believe the Communists were serious. The bussing continued until a few days later when

[12] *The Viet Cong and Children*, United States Mission to Vietnam (Saigon), p. 16

the same team stopped the same bus, took off a little girl and cut off her fingers. The school has been closed since.'[13]

On occasion the Viet Cong has deliberately set out to punish uncooperative elements of the population by the use of terror tactics resulting in the death of unarmed civilians, not in dozens, but in hundreds. Two of the most extreme examples of these sort of incidents have taken place at Dak Son in the central Highlands and in the area of the old Imperial Capital of Hue.

The victims of the Dak Son incident were a group of Montagnard Tribesmen who had fled from a Viet Cong-occupied area to settle on territory under Government control. Here they were mercilessly attacked by an infiltrating Viet Cong unit, both to punish them for deserting 'liberated' territory, and under the pretext that they had failed to provide the Viet Cong with recruits or porters. The Viet Cong force used flame throwers in their attack; and the newly-built undefended village was burnt to the ground. More than 200 villagers were killed, and hundreds of others were badly burnt or wounded by splinters from the grenades which were thrown into the ditches in which they had tried to take shelter.

The incidents in Hue after the temporary fall of the city to the Communist forces and during the Tet Offensive were probably the most savage of the entire war, although attracting astonishingly little publicity in the outside world.

After the fall of the city to the Communists, civilian cadres of the NLF, acting to a pre-arranged plan and accompanied by execution squads, toured the streets with lists of the names and addresses of various categories of 'enemies of the revolution'. These were arrested and taken before a special tribunal, which held sway in the courtyard of a building used as Communist headquarters. Their public 'trials' lasted only about ten minutes and so far as is known there were no cases of any being found not guilty. Punishment was invariably immediate execution. The 'undesirable' elements liquidated in this way included military and police officers, civil servants, school teachers, members of religious groups, and selected persons prominent in the life of the city with an influence on public opinion.

With the tide of battle running strong in the Viet Cong's

13 IV Corps Advisers' Official Report (1969)

favour in the first days of the Offensive, and spurred on by constant statements from headquarters that total victory was imminent, the occupiers of Hue became convinced that their hold upon the city would be permanent. Consequently they started to act with even greater fervour to stamp out the influence of the Saigon Government and to destroy the 'imperialist' social order they had found. Orders were issued to round up all 'social negatives', a term apparently meant to include all groups or individuals who represented any form of even potential danger to the social system it was intended to impose. Looming large amongst these were members of political parties, priests, both Catholic and Buddhist, members of social groups and movements, intellectuals, and even pro-Communist students who happened to have upper- or middle-class backgrounds.

Increasingly, this new round-up came to take the form not of arrest but of instant execution without explanation in the victim's own homes: it often meant the destruction of entire families.

In one well-authenticated case an execution squad arrived at the home of an active community leader and proceeded to shoot him, his wife, his son and daughter-in-law, his own daughter, a husband and wife couple the family had employed as servants, and their baby. The work of destruction did not stop even there; the murdered family's cat was strangled, their dog clubbed to death, and goldfish scooped out of a bowl and thrown on the floor.

The atrocities did not, however, reach their terrible climax until the battle in the Hue area began to turn in favour of the Government forces. Once it became apparent to the Viet Cong that it was only a matter of time before they were forced out of the city a new round-up seems to have commenced. But this time the victims included anyone whom it was thought might be able to identify key figures in the Communist underground who had 'surfaced' during the uprising; or who were otherwise in a position to provide the returning Government and American forces with valuable information.

Those now brought in, together with several thousand others ostensibly being held for 'political re-education', were marched out of the city by their captors; to this day few have been seen alive again. Instead, during the eighteen months following the return of Government forces, a whole series of mass graves were

93

discovered in the beautiful countryside surrounding the city. At Gia Hoi High School on the city's outskirts, which had been used as a detention centre by the Viet Cong and where mass executions of prisoners took place night after night, 170 bodies were found buried in pits in the school grounds; and in the almost inaccessible Da Mai creek, deep in jungle-covered hills some miles away, the bones of several hundred people were discovered strewn along the bed of a stream.

By 1970 over 3,500 bodies had been discovered, most of them identified as missing citizens of Hue; and some even provided evidence of their burial alive. At the same time it was estimated that at least a further 2,000 people were still unaccounted for. The largest mass graves discovered were found in a stretch of silvery sand dunes by the edge of the South China Sea. Some 800 bodies were recovered from this one area. Here a line of shallow depressions in the sand marking the site of the graves, and a sinister litter of spent submachine-gun cartridge cases and loops of now-withered rice straw, used to tie the victims' hands, gives mute but all too convincing evidence of the dark and grim turn events might still take throughout South Vietnam, should the long-drawn-out and tragic struggle in Vietnam finally end in victory for the revolutionaries of the Viet Cong and their Hanoi controllers.

CHAPTER V

The New Revolutionaries of the West

By the end of the 1960s the various revolutionary groups which had first appeared or emerged from the shadows in the early years of the decade were coming into even greater prominence. To an increasing extent they were in many fields outpacing the orthodox Communist parties in ardour and militancy, although the organizational techniques and political flair of the former in general remained superior.

The picture presented was a constantly changing one, with new groups forming, splitting, or sometimes disbanding: a jumbled pattern of Maoists, Trotskyists, anarchists, 'Revolutionary Socialists' and pro-Cuban elements strenuously competing for the allegiance of the discontented, the embittered, or the young and idealistic, but all with an equal determination to work for the destruction of present-day Western society through a revolutionary upheaval, which some saw as coming sooner, some later, but all as inevitable.

As before, much of their activity remained centred upon bringing about 'the radicalization' of Western youth, and upon the building of 'Red Universities' as bases for future revolutionary activity. The concept of this strategy was defined as:

'The University ought to be transformed from a factory, producing robots, into an organizing centre for anti-capitalist activities, a powerhouse for revolutionary education, an arena for mobilizing youth in a struggle for the complete transformation of society.'[1]

Even the disappearance of the West German Sozialischer Deutscher Studentenbund and the American Students for a Democratic Society, who supplied much of the impetus for the original surge of revolutionary student activity, has failed to significantly slacken this offensive against the present system of higher education which the revolutionaries regard as a particularly soft target.

The student-based 'revolution' of May 1968 in Paris provided both encouragement and a salutary lesson to the new revolutionaries of the West. Encouragement in it seemed to provide proof that popular revolt was still a practical possibility, a lesson in that although the social and governmental machine of a major capitalist state had been made to visibly tremble, it was obvious in the end that considerably more thorough preparatory work was needed to undermine the whole structure sufficiently to bring it crashing to the ground.

The twin effects of this fateful French spring was to cause the new revolutionaries both to redouble their efforts, and (with the exception of the anarchists, the very nature of whose philosophy makes them averse to sophisticated organization and united effort, and one other category which will be mentioned later) to concentrate an increasing part of their activities on building a firm base in the form of 'revolutionary parties'. At the same time an intensive campaign of propaganda and psychological warfare has been opened, directed at popularizing the revolutionary cause and softening up 'the establishment' and upholders of 'the system' to the point where they are no longer willing to offer serious resistance to the revolutionaries' demands.

In Britain the last three years has seen a marked stepping up in the efforts of the new revolutionaries to foment industrial unrest and to turn the trade unions into 'revolutionary instruments'. There has, as a result, been a noticeable increase in the influence of (in particular) Trotskyist revolutionaries amongst the ranks of militant trade unionists, and in some fields of union activity their influence is now at least on a par with, or even starting to surpass, that of the much longer established and more

[1] *Red Mole* (May, 1972)

experienced industrial cadres of the Communist Party of Great Britain.

This activity came more and more into prominence during the mounting campaign against the Conservative Government's Industrial Relations Act during the latter part of 1971 and throughout 1972. Prominent in this campaign have been the Trotskyist-aligned International Socialists and the International Marxist Group, both of which had previously been active in the universities and in such campaigns as the organization and management of anti-American demonstrations over Vietnam.

Nearly 700 delegates attended an industrial conference held by the International Socialists in Manchester at the end of January 1972. Amongst those present were car workers, electricians, engineers, busmen, miners, dockers, printers, post office engineers and power workers. A resolution was passed calling for total opposition to the Industrial Relations Act and the overthrow of the Conservative Government. Some evidence of the International Socialists' methods of industrial agitation came to light in the course of an investigation by *Daily Mail* reporters into the activities of a group of young teachers, all International Socialists, who were said to be 'plotting industrial chaos on Merseyside' in the summer of 1972. The reporters stated that three teachers headed a committee which aimed at establishing agitational cells in every major factory in the area. The parents of a boy studying at a local technical school said that he had first been given International Socialist literature by a teacher, and then, in his father's words, had been 'steadily drawn deeper and deeper into the IS world of subversion'.[2] The boy's father alleged that local members of the International Socialists would call for him as early as six in the morning to take him off to join picket lines outside the gates of factories where strikes were in progress.

A leading member of the International Socialists in the area admitted to the reporter that the boy had indeed been picked up very early in the morning to take part in such activity before going to school, saying: 'Anyone joining IS has to work, we have no room for passengers.'[2]

Membership of the International Socialists has increased markedly of late, and there are now thirty-three branches in the

[2] *East-West Digest*, No. 13, July 1972

Greater London and Home Counties area alone. Its industrial activities are under the direction of Roger Rosewell, formerly a trade union official in the Midlands. A special fighting fund has been established to raise money to allow for the employment of more full-time organizers in industry.

International Socialists are active in agitation in the electrical supply industry. A special paper, *Advance*, described as being the 'rank and file power workers' newspaper', is published. This publication has pointed out that: 'The electricity supply industry is the most important in the country. When it stops producing so do 95 per cent of all other industries. The effects of a simple work to rule and overtime ban by the manual workers in the industry caused nationwide industrial dislocation.'[3]

A special booklet for power supply workers, entitled *The Power Game* and published by the International Socialist-controlled Pluto Press, calls for the building of a united front between miners and power workers and has been described by Wally Preston, editor of *Advance*, as 'an effective weapon to be used by electricity supply workers in their day-to-day struggles at their various locations'.

The International Socialists have also been making considerable efforts for some appreciable time to establish influence within various white-collar unions, here again not without some success. Their particular targets have been the National Union of Teachers, the National Union of Journalists, and the National Association of Local Government Officers. IS's attempts to influence teachers are made partly through a monthly magazine, *Rank and File for Teachers*, which first appeared in 1968, and with which Mrs Anneta Gluckstein, wife of Ygael Gluckstein (otherwise known as Tony Cliff), the leading IS theoretician, is closely connected.

One of the main messages of this publication is the need to 'demoralize' the schools, and it has called for the establishment of staff councils which will take all important decisions instead of leaving them to the headmaster. The need to establish such councils has been described in *Rank and File* as being crucial if the effort 'to produce some cracks in the authoritarian structure is to succeed'. One member of its editorial board is on record as

3 *East-West Digest*, No. 12, June 1972

98

saying that: '*Rank and File* has always supported in principle the "pupil power movement" such as SAU [Schools Action Union].'[4] The paper has attacked:

'Vicious divisions between teacher and child, the competitiveness, the examination system, the unscrupulous exploitation of children to serve in a social machine they do not control—lessons soon learnt from the criteria of the wider society outside school.'[4]

Special poems by children often appear in the pages of *Rank and File*. One that appeared in the Spring of 1972 by a girl of thirteen, resident in Islington, entitled 'Stephen McCarthy's Death—The System' and illustrated with a picture of a policeman with a drawn truncheon, began with the words:

'Arrested with violence, that's the Law:
Battered and bleeding on a Police cell floor,
Begging for help at Death's door,
But that's the system, nothing more.'[4]

Agitation along the lines indicated in *Rank and File* is promoted through *Rank and File* teachers' support groups built around readers of the magazine in a large number of centres, including London, Birmingham, Bradford, Cambridge, Coventry, Durham, Exeter, Sheffield, Southampton, Swansea and York. It was members of such groups who organized a walk-out at the Annual General Meeting of the National Union of Teachers in 1972, just before the Minister of Education was about to address the assembly. And *Rank and File* teachers' groups have particularly strong influence in the Association for Teachers in Technical Institutions.

International Socialists mostly agitate amongst local Government employees through a special group set up to recruit members for IS from the National Association of Local Government Officers (NALGO), and known as the NALGO Action Group. Their activities are especially directed at recruiting support from amongst county and town hall staffs.

In the area of news media, IS influence is marked in the National Union of Journalists' important Magazine and Book Branch which operates from the Union's London headquarters. The Branch committee includes members with sympathies for

[4] *East-West Digest*, No. 14, July 1972

99

both the International Socialists and the Communist Party of Great Britain. It issues its own monthly publication edited by Roger Protz, who is also editor of the main IS journal, *Socialist Worker*. Another prominent International Socialist who has had close connection with the branch is Paul Foot, a former member of the staff of *Private Eye*.

Another organization concerned with the presentation of news, and with which prominent International Socialists concern themselves, is the Free Communications Group (FCG). The aims of the FCG can be summarized as being the social ownership of the means of communication, together with a comprehensive change in the present nature of our society. It has made no bones about its belief that the press, radio, television services and the cinema industry should be controlled by the employees who actually work for these concerns.

In the group's first pamphlet, *In Place of Management: I—The Press*, a plan is discussed for the establishment of the 'democratic control' of British newspapers. It is suggested that journalists should share in editorial and managerial control, and that this should include the power to make and veto appointments, including that of the Editor. According to the pamphlet the ultimate aim should be that 'those who make the paper own it'. The FCG also aims at mounting a campaign for the introduction of 'democratic media'.

Although formed by a very small number of left-wing journalists it has now grown to a membership of almost 700, and its activities cover all sections of the news media. A correspondent of the *Lancashire Evening Telegraph*, on the 11 January 1971, described how one of the authors of the FCG pamphlet referred to above described to him how 'The FCG spreads the gospel of democratic control to journalists in newspapers, TV, and radio. He told me that the FCG toured the country holding meetings for journalists in Edinburgh, Glasgow, Newcastle, Stockton, Manchester, Liverpool, Birmingham, Bristol, Nottingham, and Brighton.'

The Free Communications Group's ability to expand its activities has obviously been considerably eased by the provision of a grant by the Rowntree Trust of the sum of £6,000, spread over three years, and the provision of office accommodation and secretarial assistance. The group publishes its own magazine, *The Open Secret*, which for a time was published from the same address as that of the International Socialist's publishing outlet, the Socialist Review Publishing Company. Among the well-known figures from the world of news media who are or have been members of the FCG's Central Committee occur the names of Stuart Hood, a former BBC programmes controller, and the editor of Granada Television's programme *World In Action*, Gus MacDonald, Claude Cockburn, a member of the staff of *Private Eye* and formerly Diplomatic Correspondent of *The Daily Worker*, and the Chairman of the National Union of Journalists Magazine and Book Branch, Eric Winter. Actual policy-making appears to be in the hands of a small steering Committee meeting weekly.

Since the FCG's current membership is tiny in proportion to that of the National Union of Journalists, it would appear that the group bases its hopes of bringing influence to bear in the Union largely on assuming control of individual newspaper offices' chapels; a task which could be eased by the disinclination of the majority of journalists to take part in Union affairs. Once, of course, power is assumed, militants can then ask for a say in the running of the offices.

Recently, a number of reports have appeared about the pressure applied by International Socialists on the journalistic staff of such publications as the *Sunday Times Magazine*, *Private Eye*, and the industrial newspaper *Construction News* over matters of editorial and other policy. Reports in the early part of 1972 spoke of a determined attempt being prepared by IS sympathizers to take over *Private Eye*. A protracted, and, as far as the militants were concerned, unsuccessful struggle for control of *Construction News* had its roots largely in the left-wing and, in some cases, IS sympathies, of the membership of several of the staff who have now left the magazine, some of whom held important positions. At one point an attempt was even made to force a code of conduct on the Editor, which included a demand for joint staff consultation with him on all matters of importance; a demand very reminiscent of that put forward as one of the main planks of the policy of the Free Communications Group.

In the film industry, International Socialists seek to exert influence through the militant members of the Association of Cinematograph, Television, and Allied Technicians (ACTT), or through so-called Members Action Committees of the British Film Institute.

The International Socialists also provide a good example of the amount of propaganda material produced by some Western revolutionary organizations. In addition to the weekly paper *Socialist Worker*, which claims a circulation of 27,000, and the other publications already mentioned above, IS publishes a special magazine for militants in the building industry, called *Building Workers Charter*, two magazines for workers in the engineering and electrical industries, *Rank and File Engineer* and *Grading and Contracting Sparks*, and a quarterly theoretical journal, *International Socialism*.

On top of all these the movement's publishing company produces a large number of pamphlets and leaflets. Its presses have been used for the production of propaganda for distribution in Northern Ireland, as well as for various special papers intended for distribution amongst trades unionists involved in industrial disputes, for example *The Carworker*, which made its appearance in many motor industry centres in the spring of 1971, or *The Socialist Docker* which was being distributed in a number of ports in the summer of 1970.

In common with all other revolutionary groups in Britain, the International Socialists give great attention to the Civil Rights Association and to the revolutionary organization of People's Democracy, as well as consistent, if sometimes more qualified support to the IRA. IS ties with People's Democracy have always been particularly close since the foundation of the latter in 1969, and that best-known of all leading figures in People's Democracy, Miss Bernadette Devlin, MP, has been a frequent contributor to the pages of *Socialist Worker*.

A development of great importance affecting revolutionary movements in the West has been the re-emergence of the Trotskyist IV International, first formed before the 1939–45 War at the instigation of Trotsky himself, and dormant for many years after his death. Its headquarters are now located in Brussels, and it has affiliated organizations in Britain, France, and other Western European countries, as well as in India, Ceylon, Japan and Latin America. In 1971 an affiliated group was established in Dublin, and the IV International follows a policy of strong support for the IRA, and has strong links with the Provisionals.

In the spring of 1972 the well-known revolutionary agitator, Tariq Ali, a leading member of the IV International's British affiliate, the International Marxist Group (IMG), entered France illegally to take part in a press conference organized by the International in Paris. Beside him on the platform were Ernest Mandel, a prominent Belgian Trotskyist, and the International's Secretary-General, Alain Krivine, leader of its French affiliate, the Communist League, who played a leading role in the events of May 1968 in the French capital. During the course of the conference, Tariq Ali said that Ireland's entry into the Common Market would mean the war between Ireland and Britain would continue on a European scale.

Other well-known leaders of the International Marxist Group include Robin Blackburn, the sociology lecturer who was dismissed from his post at the London School of Economics because of his political activities, Pat Jordan, and Bob Purdie. For a considerable time the group has largely controlled the Vietnam Solidarity Campaign, an organization which in recent years has sponsored most of the large-scale demonstrations against American participation in the war in Vietnam.

Like the International Socialists, the International Marxists have recently been devoting an increasing amount of their activity to industrial agitation. A special supplement to the group's paper, *Red Mole*, on 'Building The IV International In Britain', has claimed that 'The IMG has begun to work systematically and gain members at least in the mines, the car industry, the building industry, among the unemployed, the steel industry, in transport and various white collar unions.'

An article in *Red Mole* on 13 March 1972 stated 'But whatever the outcome of the heartsearchings and manoeuvres of the bourgeoisie, the basic tasks of working-class militants in the economic struggle must remain the same: to smash any wage freeze in whatever guise and under whoever's sponsorship, to make the Industrial Relations Act unusable; and to redouble solidarity action for any section of workers on strike.'

IMG militants have worked hard in the building industry, and have actively supported the Charter Group, which under Communist leadership coordinated the strike action which brought work on building sites to a halt in the summer of 1972. The IMG has been pressing for a campaign to 'democratize' the building trade unions through pressure from 'site committees' holding regular meetings.

Like the International Socialists, the IMG places considerable emphasis on activity amongst school teachers, a field in which it claims some success. An article in *Red Mole* of 17 April 1972 maintained that 'Our teacher caucus is almost as large as all our other union caucuses combined. Our teacher comrades should utilize the trades union avenues open to them to popularize and promote our fundamental transitional programme for the creation of a class-struggle left wing in the unions.'

The International Marxist Group has published a pamphlet on the steel industry, entitled *Steel, The Coming Redundancies and How to Fight Them*. In this it is suggested that the first step to ward off redundancies in the industry should be the formation of action committees whose role should be to agitate and organize the 'backward' rank and file. A conference should be held to launch a newspaper on an industry-wide scale, and following this 'local struggles' should be launched which could snowball into a major campaign affecting the whole industry.

A particular IMG activity in connection with trade union work is support for Claimants Unions. The National Federation of Claimants Unions made its appearance at a conference in Birmingham in March 1970. A charter was drawn up to govern the aims of each union, which, it was agreed, should be to secure

1   The right to an adequate income without a means test for all people.
2   A free welfare state, for all, with its services controlled by the people who use it.
3   No secrets and the right to full information.
4   No distinction between so-called 'deserving' and 'undeserving' cases.

In a booklet put out by the National Federation of Claimants Unions especially for the information of strikers and entitled *Strikers and Supplementary Benefits*, the National Federation of

Claimants Unions urges all workers' organizations to press for supplementary benefits for strikers, as well as for their families, as of right and without a means test. It also calls upon all Civil Service Unions to refuse to implement any measures designed to deny strikers supplementary benefits, and asks workers to be ready to take mass strike action in support of workers denied strike benefits. It is, therefore, not surprising to find the IMG's *Red Mole* stating that—'it is vital that as revolutionaries we be involved in the struggle to build these unions';[5] or pointing out that 'supplementary benefit is a vital source of income to strikers', and that 'organized pressure' on the part of Claimants Unions can be, and in fact already has been, an important factor in obtaining strike benefits from reluctant social security services.

The International Marxist Group has defined its main role as being to build 'a revolutionary cadre force in Britain. This means building a body of opinion which is prepared to use revolutionary violence in Britain to overthrow the British ruling class.'

As well as its London headquarters, from which large quantities of propaganda material are produced on modern presses and from which a large variety of campaigns are run, the group also maintains a bookshop in Nottingham. This has been used as a coordinating centre for picketing activities during major strikes. The IMG seeks to expand its strength partly through using *Red Mole* as a 'collective organizer', and partly through 'Red Circles', or groups of activist readers of the paper, established in many parts of the country. The group is keen to attract young people through its Spartacus League youth movement, and it also has a special women's section. It is active amongst militants of the immigrant community; its vociferous support for the IRA is based upon the view that the struggle in Ireland is inseparably bound up with coming events in mainland Britain. In his book *The Coming British Revolution*, Tariq Ali has written:

> 'The need for British revolutionists to solidarize with the Irish struggle is therefore paramount. They must support the armed action of Irish republicanism against British imperialism in public. They must attempt to build a solidarity campaign which can win Irish workers over in

5 *East-West Digest*, No. 9, May 1972

105

large numbers and radicalize them ... The methods which are being used in Ireland are not new to that country, where guerrilla warfare was born, but they have succeeded in shaking the complacency of any in Britain who have been a bit taken aback that an armed struggle involving thousands of British soldiers can take place just across the water. The Irish workers, who in this respect have a memory which the British working class lacks, could be decisive in bringing these traditions into the heart of industrial Britain. One can visualize a situation within the next few years where a city like Liverpool could witness an armed insurrection by sections of the proletariat.'[6]

The third and longest-established of the Trotskyist groups in Britain, the Socialist Labour League, has for long concentrated most of its activity upon the recruitment of young workers through work in the trade unions. Like the two other groups mentioned, it is doing its utmost to exploit existing industrial tensions, and at the beginning of 1972 it organized a number of 'right to work' marches on London. According to the League's Director, Gerald Healey, these had the purpose of building up the strength of the League and its Young Socialist youth movement in order to enable it to play its part as the central force in a campaign to bring about the collapse of the Conservative Government.

THEORY INTO PRACTICE

The first of the newly emerging revolutionaries of North America and Western Europe seriously to begin to plan the tactical and strategic methods by which Western society could be destroyed by means of armed insurrection appear to have been the Black Power groups of the United States. As early as 1964, for instance, Robert Williams, leader of the Revolutionary Action Movement, one of the most militant of such bodies, was writing of a new concept of 'lightning campaigns', conducted by revolutionaries in highly sensitive urban communities, and with the resulting confusion and chaos then spreading to the surrounding countryside—a total reversal of the well-established theories

[6] Tariq Ali, *The Coming British Revolution*, Jonathan Cape (London, 1972), pp. 229–30

of major prophets of revolutionary war such as Che Guevara and Mao Tse-tung.

Williams explained the reasons for this reversal by saying that the old methods of guerrilla warfare, waged in the hills and countryside, would stand no chance in a well-developed country such as the USA. Any force which tried such methods would, he considered, be quickly wiped out. The new concept, Williams said, was to:

'huddle as close to the enemy as possible so as to neutralize his modern and fierce weapons. The new concept creates conditions that involve the total community whether they want to be involved or not. It sustains a state of confusion and destruction of property. It dislocates the organs of harmony and order and reduces central power to the level of a helpless sprawling octopus. During the hours of day sporadic rioting takes place, and massive sniping. Night brings all-out warfare, organized fighting and unlimited terror against the oppressor and his forces.'

Williams hoped that his new concept would create a situation in which:

'The USA will become a bedlam of confusion and chaos, the factory workers will be afraid to venture out on the streets to report to their jobs. The telephone workers and radio workers will be afraid to report. Stores will be destroyed and looted. Property will be damaged and expensive buildings will be reduced to ashes. Essential pipelines will be blown up and all manner of sabotage will occur. Violence and terror will spread like a firestorm.'[7]

In order to put his theories of urban insurrection into practice Williams suggested the formation of a black revolutionary organization which would be divided into three sections. The first of these sections would consist of armed 'self-defence squads', operating openly. The second type of detachment would comprise undercover guerrilla groups who would operate against the police during riots. The third category would consist of squads specializing in the use of sabotage and arson.

These sabotage squads should be formed from members who could pose as 'moderates' in order to gain access to high security

[7] *Revolution*, March 1964

zones, their particular targets being transport and communication centres in large cities, public buildings, and military installations. They should also be used as teams of mobile fire-raisers, carrying out acts of arson over wide areas in order to 'elicit panic and a feeling of impending doom'.[8]

The Black Panthers, who came to dominate the American Black Power movement, although believing in the need for an ultimate revolution and an alliance between Black Power, white revolutionaries, and the revolutionaries of the Third World, and issuing extremely threatening, not to say blood-thirsty literature, have not so far resorted to organized armed action (although individual members have been involved in terrorist incidents), believing that the time for successful revolution is not yet ripe. At the present time the movement has in fact become deeply split between those who wish to continue concentrating upon preparations for launching a campaign of guerrilla warfare, and those who believe the best way forward lies in working within 'the system' for the time being. Despite the hopes of such leaders as Williams and the incipient threat of 'black ghetto revolt', the first use of anti-Government terrorism on a country-wide scale has come from a quite different direction.

By 1969, the Students for a Democratic Society were riven by disputes between Maoist and other factions and many of its more violent-minded members were becoming increasingly impatient for more dramatic forms of action than campus demonstrations and sit-ins, however militant or well-organized. From the welter of argument at an SDS conference in June of that year there emerged a splinter group, aiming to impress the seriousness of America's young revolutionaries in no uncertain way. The leader of this new group was Mark Rudd, formerly leader of the SDS Chapter at Columbia University; where his activities had caused the university's president to describe him as being highly dangerous and completely unscrupulous.

The name taken by the new group was that of 'the Weathermen', a title suggested by lines in a song by Bob Dylan, *Subterranean Homesick Blues*, which runs, 'You don't need a weatherman to know which way the wind blows'. It was committed to the belief that the 'world-wide monster of American

[8] *Revolution*, March 1964

Imperialism' was the main cause of all the ills of the time, and that the destruction of this 'monster' should be the first aim of the fast-approaching world-wide revolution, which American youth must do all in its power to aid.

The first major action of the group took place on 8 October 1969 in Chicago. Here the Weathermen, many dressed in full street-fighting gear, equipped with helmets and staves, assembled in Lincoln Park to mark the anniversary of the death of Che Guevara and also that of a North Vietnamese Communist leader. Their proceedings took the form of a violent rampage through the fashionable Gold Coast district of the City, smashing car and shop windows, lighting fires and attacking policemen. This first 'Day of Rage' was followed by other similar efforts. The object was apparently to give the Weathermen the image of being fearless fighters against the 'forces of oppression', and so gain support from a wide range of radical opinion. In fact with public opinion already rapidly tiring of scenes of confrontation between demonstrators and police, and in this case the obvious aggressive intent of the latter, the effect was almost wholly counter-productive.

At this early stage in their existence the Weathermen also engaged in various propaganda exercises, such as sudden descents on high schools, and attempts to gather audiences by holding impromptu meetings on holiday beaches.

Members of the organization took to living in what were termed 'affinity groups', in effect communes of usually ten or twelve people. A defector has described the form life took in one of these groups in Detroit. The group barricaded itself inside an abandoned house which was deliberately kept in a state of untended squalor. Life was spartan, although every now and then there were orgies with free use of drugs and alcohol, commodities which were normally banned.

In order to train themselves for the rigours of their revolutionary campaign, members would sometimes go without food or sleep for days. An important part of their self-imposed training were exercises designed to eliminate respect for 'bourgeois morality'; on one occasion such an exercise included wrecking tombstones in a nearby cemetery in order to try to eradicate respect for the dead.

In another incident the group caught, killed and ate an alley cat, apparently both to satisfy their hunger and apparently to try to instil a savage ruthlessness in themselves. Training included long sessions of 'self-criticism' and instruction in handling explosives and firearms.

Most of the Weathermen's leading figures have come from comfortable wealthy homes. Often they are the children of parents with distinguished careers in business or the professions, and prominent in local communities: and often themselves the possessors of considerable academic qualifications. A case in point is that of Bernadette Dorhn, who may now have succeeded Mark Rudd as head of the Weathermen's underground network. The twenty-eight-year-old daughter of rich parents with a pleasant home in the popular Oak Park suburb of Chicago, she had a record as a brilliant student at Chicago Law School, from which she emerged with a doctorate. Within quite a short time of doing so, however, she had become notorious as a fanatical young revolutionary with extremely violent opinions. She became one of the leaders of the cult of admiration for the Manson gang that affected many Weathermen. Describing her feelings of exaltation on hearing news of the murders she is said to have exclaimed: 'Like wow! it blew my mind.' At one time some Weathermen wanted to adopt a four-fingered salute as a recognition signal as a token of respect for Manson's action in digging a fork into the stomach of one of his victims.

In December 1969, the Weathermen decided to abandon all legal political operations, to go underground, and to commence upon a campaign of terrorism. The 'affinity groups' were abandoned and the movement split up into three- or four-member cells, receiving orders and keeping in touch through the mail, telephone, and by means of 'dead letter drops'.

The aim of the terrorist campaign was to create chaos in the main centres of population and so bring about a situation which would make 'mass public action' leading to revolution possible. However, no lists of strategic targets were drawn up, cells being supposed to operate largely on their own initiative as opportunities presented themselves. Once the campaign got under way, a sort of status system seems to have come into existence, with members being graded according to their willingness to take part in planting bombs. During the next year the number of bombings in America soared to an average of three a day, a proportion, but by no means all, being the work of the Weathermen. Other revolutionary groups with titles such as 'Revolutionary Force 9', or the 'Volunteers of America' were in the field. Banks, large company offices, Government offices, and Police headquarters were favourite targets for attack, together with university and high school buildings.

The Weathermen did not confine themselves to bomb attacks alone. One of their more sensational exploits was the release of a leading advocate of the free use of drugs, Dr Timothy Leary, from prison and subsequently his smuggling out of the country. Another Weathermen cell embarked upon a plan to obtain access to biological weapons by blackmailing an army lieutenant involved in guarding their storage place at Fort Detrick, Maryland. The scheme's purpose was to drop the material so obtained into the water supply of a large American city to cause a period of infection.

The Weathermen's campaign suffered a major setback when a house in Greenwich Village being used as a bomb factory blew up as the result of an accident, causing several fatal casualties in their ranks and the loss of large quantities of explosives and bomb-making equipment. Found in the ruins were a number of nail bombs, an anti-personnel weapon of a type later to be used with effect in Northern Ireland. It is typical of the affluent background of many Weathermen terrorists that the house destroyed was one owned by the parents of a girl member of the organization, who had borrowed it for use as an arsenal without their knowledge whilst they were holidaying in the West Indies.

The effectiveness of the Weathermen's campaign was also considerably militated against by the movement's growing interest in drugs, evidenced by one of their communiqués, which contained the following passage:

'Drugs like LSD, like the herbs and cactus and mushrooms of the American Indians and countless civilizations that have existed on this planet, will help us to make a future world where it will be possible to live in peace.'

Probably the Weathermen's total membership has always remained under 1,000; although, as seems normal with this type of organization, there is probably a considerably larger supporters' group. Some of their attacks were responsible for considerable material damage, but by the end of 1970 many members were having serious doubts about the effectiveness of their tactics; like members of 'The People's Will' long before them they seemed to be learning that it takes more than scattered bomb explosions to destroy the fabric of a powerful state. The movement is now said to be going through a period of re-appraisal.

Few leading Weathermen have so far been arrested, despite their high place on the FBI's 'most wanted' list, although some, including Bernadette Dorhn herself, have been forced to seek refuge outside the United States.

The existence of a further white revolutionary group actively engaged in preparations for armed revolt in the USA, and with a somewhat more sophisticated approach than that of the Weathermen, was revealed as the result of researches by a member of the staff of the *San Francisco Examiner* in the Spring of 1969. The group, known as the Revolutionary Union, was a somewhat élitist organization composed of picked ex-members of such organizations as the SDS and the Maoist Progressive Labour Party. One of its founders was Professor H. Franklin of Stanford University, an active Maoist. Other leading members were Robert Avakian, a former revolutionary student at Berkeley, and Steve Hamilton whose political activities caused him to be expelled from Berkeley University in 1966. The group issued a manifesto which called for the carrying out of various forms of struggle. These included a propaganda campaign, the formation of front organizations, the use of infiltration tactics, mass demonstrations, and the raising of funds through the imposition of levies on capitalist-owned businesses.

Similar was the manifesto of the Canadian FLQ (Front de Liberation du Québec), which stressed that a revolutionary party should be able to engage in all such tactics whilst at the same time conducting a guerrilla campaign. Although it was stated that the FLQ intended to put up candidates at elections, it was made abundantly clear that this would be purely for publicity and propaganda purposes, and that any thought of obtaining power through the ballot box was completely rejected. The policy should be to steer members towards objectives that could not be obtained without revolution. A very important aim was the mounting of repeated large-scale demonstrations in order to produce an atmosphere of crisis and force the Government into unpopular repressive measures.

A number of Marxist intellectuals were amongst the prime formulators of this policy, one of them a lecturer at McGill University. The central aim of the FLQ and FLQ political activity became to build a united front of progressive forces in Quebec. To this end the use of infiltration tactics was deemed particularly important, especially when attempting to manipulate trade unions, citizen groups and youth groups, the last being used to demonstrate against the English nature of the educational system. These efforts were not without avail, contact was made with and sometimes influence gained in a considerable number of political and semi-political organizations. These included student associations and the National Federation of Trade Unions.

At one stage the theorists of this French-Canadian revolutionary movement produced a 'revolutionary scenario', setting out in full how in their view a period of intensive agitation could lead to a major political and economic crisis in the province of Quebec, which would produce the right conditions for armed revolt.

The third campaign of armed action by FLQ cells, which culminated in the kidnapping of the British diplomat James Cross and the Quebec Minister, Laporte, and the subsequent murder of the latter, commenced in 1969. Targets for bomb attacks included banks, the home of the Mayor of Montreal, and the Montreal Stock Exchange visitors' gallery, where more than twenty people were injured. Revulsion against the brutal murder of Mr Laporte and the kidnapping of Mr Cross in 1970 caused a major fall in support for the movement. At the same time Prime Minister Trudeau's use of wartime security regulations and of troops to aid the police in search and arrest operations disrupted its organization and caused its remaining members to desist from further acts of violence, at least for the time being. It is not believed, however, that the movement has been altogether extinguished.

The FLQ is known to have had links with the Black Panthers in the United States. At one time a special committee was formed by some of the intellectuals associated with it for the purpose of translating and distributing propaganda literature produced by the Black Panthers. There has also been evidence of contact with Palestinian guerrilla movements. Two FLQ members were seen and interviewed in the training camp of one such organization in Jordan in August 1970. Somewhat grimly they described the purpose of their visit to be that of learning to kill rather than to study organizational work.

In West Germany, a small but active group of urban guerrillas has substantially added to the problems of that country's police force for some time. Early last year some 2,000 policemen were employed in one search for the group's members in Hamburg. The operation involving the use of helicopters and dogs. The group was involved in shooting incidents with the police in six different German towns over a period of two years, during which time it is thought to have amassed funds amounting to at least £50,000 through bank robberies and other thefts. Subsequently, it resorted to bomb attacks causing considerable damage, and some injuries and deaths.

The group, which is generally known from the names of two of its leaders as the Baader-Meinhof group, although it also uses the name of Red Army Faction (RAF), has somewhat similar origins to the Weathermen, being formed by some more extreme members of the Sozialischer Deutscher Studentenbund, mentioned earlier in this chapter. The actual incident which led to its formation was both dramatic and violent.

In April 1968 four members of the Sozialischer Deutscher Studentenbund, including Andreas Baader, a leading activist, set fire to two warehouses in Frankfurt; the costs of the damage amounted to almost £250,000. The four were arrested and brought to trial, Andreas Baader taking the opportunity of his appearance in court to make emotional statements against the Vietnamese war and 'the system', which brought him much publicity in the left-wing press. One of those most impressed by his pronouncements was Ulrike Meinhof, a revolutionary-minded young journalist who took up the cause of the four in her articles in the left-wing magazine *Konrat*.

All four charged were sentenced to three years' imprisonment. In the spring of 1970, however, Andreas Baader was rescued from his guards in a Berlin library, which he had been allowed out from prison to visit in order to do some research work, by an armed three-member 'commando' which included Ulrike Meinhoff. The commando used tear gas and grenades as well as fire-arms to effect the rescue, in the course of which two police-men and a librarian were wounded. Almost immediately after this incident the Baader-Meinhof Group came into existence. In its first communiqué it stated:

'Did the pigs really think we would leave Comrade Baader in prison for two or three years?

Did they really think we would forever fight against batons with foul eggs, against guns with stones, against machine guns with molotov cocktails. The bullets which struck Rudi (Dutschke) finished the dream of peace and non-violence. Those who don't defend themselves die, those who don't die are buried alive in prisons, in educational institutions, in slums such as Neuklin, in the stone coffins of the new estates, in full-up kindergartens and schools, in the perfectly equipped kitchens of the new estates, in unpaid luxury bedrooms. Start armed resistance NOW, help build the Red Army.'[9]

A number of members of the group are known to have gone to the Middle East, travelling via Eastern Europe, to receive training in one of the many guerrilla camps there, and to have since returned to West Germany. Like other organizations of its type it relies heavily for funds on bank robberies, and its members are responsible for at least five successful raids on banks during 1970. The group's tactics and political philosophy are based on the premise that a situation has already arisen in Western Europe in which armed revolt can be used to destroy the existing social and governmental order, but that this must also be combined with a political struggle.

A member of the group captured and placed on trial early in 1972[10] said in evidence that the group had obtained help from a number of university professors, social workers, and other intellectuals who sometimes provided refuge in their own homes.

Another and more securely based European group bent on

[9] *International Times*
[10] By the end of the year most of the group's leading members, including both Baader and Meinhof, were in custody. Some cells were thought to remain intact, however, possibly maintaining contact with Palestinian terrorist groups.

armed as well as political struggle, is the Basque ETA. This movement, whose formation resulted from a split in the youth organization of the Basque Nationalist Party in 1967, bases its policies, like the FLQ and the IRA, on a mixture of nationalism and revolutionary Marxism. Its tactics are fairly sophisticated, great importance being given to propaganda and agitational work as well as terrorism. It divides its operations into four sections, propaganda among the workers, 'cultural activity', political work, and military activity or terrorism. Its activities in the last embrace the use of bomb attacks, assassination, and kidnapping.

A split occurred between the purely nationalist and the Marxist factions of the movement at its congress in the autumn of 1970, as a result of which the former were expelled. Its aim now is to launch an eventual revolution throughout Spain.

Revolutionary movements in North America and Western Europe, such as those mentioned, which have already taken to the use of the gun or bomb, and those that plan to do so, have been fortified in their belief that armed revolt can be made to produce satisfactory results in sophisticated and well-developed states: and even in conditions that fall well short of being revolutionary by the standards of Marx, Lenin, and the older generation of teachers, by the considerable degree of success obtained by the Tupamaros. This movement (whose operations in Uruguay, a Latin American country where social and political conditions probably more nearly approximate to those in North America or Europe than any other country on that subcontinent) largely initiated the growing interest of Western revolutionaries in urban guerrilla warfare.

The Tupamaros, like many other present-day Latin American revolutionary movements, owe their formation to the inspiration provided to radical youth by the Cuban revolution. Enthused by Castro's success, a young law student, Raul Sendric, started to try to organize a revolutionary movement among the sugar-growing peasants of Northern Uruguay early in the 1960s. It was not long before Sendric and his few colleagues began to realize that Uruguay was no Cuba, and returning to Montevideo embarked upon a completely new policy, the tactical reasons for which they outlined in their movement's first communiqué:

'We have no impregnable strongholds in our country where

we can set up a guerrilla base, although there are places it is difficult to attack. On the other hand, we have an enormous city that contains more than 300 kilometres of streets and buildings, ideal for the growth of an urban struggle.'[11]

That the Tupamaros had solid grounds indeed for placing the emphasis on the importance of urban struggle can be seen from the fact that no less than 80 per cent of Uruguayans live in towns, and about half these live in Montevideo.

The Tupamaros take their name from that of a famous Peruvian Indian guerrilla fighter, Tupa Amaru, who campaigned against Spanish rule in the eighteenth century. Their first armed action was a raid on a rifle club in 1963. They did not, however, begin to advertise their existence by issuing communiqués until 1965, at which time it is probable the movement still consisted of less than fifty people. Five years later its membership had grown to at least 3,000, with a much larger 'supporters' group'. During this time it had brought about a considerable amount of demoralization in the police and security services, forced a comparatively liberal Government to introduce stringent and unpopular security measures, effected considerable damage to the economy, obtained widespread international publicity; and had produced such an atmosphere of instability and insecurity in the country that some observers considered the possibility of launching a formidable mass uprising was almost within its grasp.

The Tupamaros have operated in a cell system, based on four- or five-member cells. Their recruits have come mainly from amongst younger members of the middle-class and white-collar workers, although they have recently been trying to broaden their appeal so as to obtain more support from the working class, students, peasants and the armed forces.

Great attention has been paid to the use of propaganda, psychological warfare, and infiltration tactics as well as armed action. In order to beat the Government's ban on the reporting of their activities, the Tupamaros have built up a whole 'counter-media' publicity service of their own, which includes the use of a mobile radio transmitter, and the utilization of the aid of friendly radio technicians to interrupt regular broadcast programmes with

[11] *Urban Guerrillas in Latin America*, Conflict Studies, Institute for the Study of Conflict (1970), p. 13

announcements. Some of their propaganda efforts take a practical form. One Christmas Eve a Tupamaro 'Hunger Commando' hijacked a delivery van loaded with food, and distributed its contents to the poor in a slum district of Montevideo. Special efforts have been made to reveal any evidence of Government corruption or other official dishonesty, sometimes with considerable success.

The Tupamaros have done their utmost to help aggravate the country's soaring inflation and the consequent economic crisis by supporting strikes, and have launched a few special economic warfare operations of their own, such as a well-prepared scheme to wreck the tourist industry, on which the country is heavily dependent, by adopting such measures as sending threatening letters to regular foreign visitors.

Terrorism has been used selectively, but on a gradually widening scale, for the purpose of proving that the Government cannot protect its friends and of striking fear into the hearts of members of the security forces by such acts as the murder of policemen off duty. It is thought that part of the Tupamaros' success has been due to the building up of their extremely good intelligence service, which has included the recruiting of agents in the ranks of the security services, the staff of banks and other large commercial concerns, and the civil service.

The Tupamaros have links with similar revolutionary movements in Argentina, Bolivia and Brazil, and see themselves very much as members of an international revolutionary movement. Much of their international publicity has been obtained through a series of sensational kidnapping of both national and foreign VIPs, notably Sir Geoffrey Jackson of the British Embassy in Montevideo.

Whilst the activities of the Tupamaros continue to be watched with close attention by revolutionaries all over the Western world,[12] the eyes of many of them have also been straying to the developing situation in Northern Ireland.

[12] The movement met with a number of reverses at the hands of the security forces during 1972, lessening its power to cause serious disruption.

CHAPTER VI

Ireland—Shape of the Future?

One snowy winter night six young members of the Irish Republican Army landed from two small boats on the Ulster shore of Lough Foyle. Their orders were to carry out an attack with gelignite bombs on the British Army camp at Ballykelly. Even before they jumped ashore, however, it was all too apparent from the number of flares and searchlights illuminating the stormy night sky that the garrison was very much on its guard against an attack, and that the intended operation was quite impracticable.

So the small party started to tramp around with their gelignite through the falling snow flakes in search of some alternative target. Eventually the outline of a large building of seeming importance loomed up in the darkness. Carefully placing their gelignite charges at its base the party beat a hasty retreat to the boats; the dangers of their return journey across the water had considerably increased, because the sentry they had left to guard the boats let one of them drift away in his excitement at seeing his comrades return.

But the dangers and disappointment of their return trip were somewhat lightened by the flash and roar of a major explosion from the direction of their 'alternative target'. Next morning their spirits sank again when they heard that this target's military importance belonged more to the nineteenth than to the twentieth century: it being, in fact, a long derelict Martello Tower dating from the Napoleonic Wars.

It was an incident somewhat typical of the futility and

disappointing results of 'Operation Harvest', as the IRA's border campaign of 1956–62 was named. It was a campaign which included some bloody killings of Ulster policemen and did over £1 million worth of damage in the Province, but also one in which more IRA men lost their lives as the result of the premature explosion of their own bombs than fell to the bullets of the security forces; and one which attracted such negligible support from the Catholic minority in Ulster and so little support in the Irish Republic, that at its close the IRA High Command was compelled to issue a mournful statement that the minds of the Irish people appeared to have been distracted from the 'supreme issue' of the unity of their country.

The failure of the border campaign was accompanied by the dying strains of the old song of purely nationalist struggle that had been the refrain of the IRA for so long. When the gun next came back into Irish politics, it was with a new theme song, in which the old lines of religious and nationalist fervour had become strangely and ominously mixed with those of a new and different kind.

REFORMISTS AND REVOLUTIONARIES

Movements concerned with civil rights which open their ranks to all comers, regardless of political affiliations, form an ideal target for infiltration by extremists and revolutionaries, no matter how moderately intentioned their founders are or how reasonable their original aims; and in this the Civil Rights Movement of Northern Ireland has been no exception.

The Civil Rights Movement officially came into being at a public meeting in Belfast at the beginning of February 1967. It owed its origins to a group of people active in the Campaign for Social Justice in Northern Ireland, which was founded in 1964 in Dungannon, to collect and publish information about alleged injustice and religious discrimination in the Province. Its constitution was modelled on that of the National Council for Civil Liberties in Great Britain, to which it is affiliated.

The original objects of the movement as it began its public existence were manifold: the establishment of universal franchise in local elections, the redrawing of electoral boundaries, legislation against discrimination in local government and the provision of machinery to remedy grievances against local government, a compulsory points system for housing, the repeal of the Special Powers Act, and the abolition of the 'B' Specials.

Over six months before the Belfast meeting, however, another meeting, this time private, had been held in Maghera to discuss plans for the formation of the new body. This had been attended by, amongst others, Cathal Goulding, Chief of Staff of the IRA. Goulding had been enthusiastic about the plan, for whichever way it went the IRA clearly stood a chance of benefiting. If the movement went well and its demands were granted, the IRA could increase its prestige through having shown discreet support; if, on the other hand, they were refused, and this resulted in fierce political and civil strife, there would be a promising new situation for the IRA to exploit. The IRA's main theoretician, Dr Roy Johnston, was also enthusiastic about the plan, but it seems that he wanted the IRA to openly dominate the movement in a way which it never really did in the early days.

But, although not dominant, the presence of elements of the IRA, together with those of the new revolutionary left, were early apparent within its ranks. The ominous merging of the two strains that was later to produce such dire results was revealed in a police report concerning some of the leaders of the Civil Rights' second big march, that in Londonderry on 5 October 1967:

> 'Matt O'Leary is a member of the Revolutionary Socialist Alliance and a self-confessed Communist . . . George Finbarr O'Doherty, unemployed, is a Republican known to the police for about six years . . . John White is a member of the IRA . . . Eamonn Melaugh is a known Republican who applied to join the IRA as far back as 1955 (and was not accepted) . . . Eamonn McCann is a member of the Derry Labour Party, a Republican and believed to be a Communist . . . He is closely associated with Gerry Lawless . . .'[1]

The march in question produced the first major clash between Civil Rights' demonstrators and the police. The violence came not from the IRA element present, since the IRA at this stage for its own reasons was intent upon preventing violent confrontations, and indeed even on some occasions provided stewards

[1] *Sunday Times* Insight Team, *Ulster*, André Deutsch (London, 1972), p. 50

in order to try to prevent these happening, but from the ultra-left. The original idea of the march had come from a left-wing body known as the Derry Housing Action Committee, in which Eamonn McCann was active.

The history of Mr McCann is interesting. A graduate of Belfast University, where he won a prize for oratory, he subsequently worked on a number of London building sites, and became editor of *The Irish Militant*, a periodical produced by the Irish Workers' Group, a now defunct Trotskyist organization, and was subsequently to play a leading part in the organization of People's Democracy.

Violence seems to have been initiated on 5 October by members of the Young Socialist Alliance, a student group from Belfast consisting mostly of former members of the Irish Workers' Group. The Cameron Report comments that:

'The extremists of the left were anxious to ensure that there was a violent "confrontation" with the police, and to organize opposition in the city on class lines. Since these extremists have been principally responsible for the detailed organization of the march it is not surprising that there are no serious plans to control it, or to ensure that it went off peacefully.'[2]

The violence so initiated against the wishes of the leadership of the Civil Rights Movement, and the subsequent over-reaction and excessive force used by the police, made 5 October a traumatic day with far-reaching consequences.

Not the least of these consequences was the birth of People's Democracy. This grew from a meeting of students held at Belfast University to protest at the police action on 5 October. The decision to establish a separate group to work within the Civil Rights Movement was actually taken on 9 October, at a meeting addressed by Michael Farrell, who had formerly studied for the priesthood before becoming converted to revolutionary socialism, and who later came to admit, 'We don't want reform in Northern Ireland, we want a revolution.'[3]

Bernadette Devlin, who so quickly became probably the best-known member of People's Democracy in the world at large,

2 *Disturbances in Northern Ireland*, CMD 352 (1962), paragraph 46
3 *New Left Review*, April 1971

described the ten members of its first committee as being 'the weirdest looking bunch of people you ever saw'. Prominent amongst them were Kevin Boyle, a law lecturer, who was afterwards to state that he saw the Paris uprising of 1968 as having a great influence on the plan of action pursued by People's Democracy, and Cyril Toman, like Michael Farrell a former member of the Irish Workers' Group, to which a number of the rank and file of the movement had also belonged. Immediately after formation People's Democracy devoted itself to a period of intensive political study. Bernadette Devlin has remarked that during every discussion more and more people seemed to be drawn further and further left. Cyril Toman was People's Democracy's main theoretician at this time, and was fond of reading long quotations of Marx to the assembled students.

People's Democracy, however, did not confine itself to political self-education for long. Growing links soon became evident with such movements as the Revolutionary Socialists' Students Federation in London, and in particular with the Trotskyist-aligned International Socialists, who provided important aid in the form of propaganda literature produced on its London presses. Funds also began to find their way to 'PD', as it became known, some from the students' councils of some English universities.

PD emerged from its period of discussion dedicated to the establishment of a Workers' Socialist Republic throughout Ireland. In the words of the Cameron report, it now constituted a 'small but tightly-knit group', whose frankly admitted intentions were to use the Civil Rights movement for their own purposes, and who were prepared and ready, when and where it suited them, to invoke and accept violence. The report found that PD represented a threat to the stability and existence of the Northern Ireland Constitution and found one of its leading members, Eamonn McCann, who like Miss Devlin became increasingly prominent at all scenes of disorder, to have been throughout this early period of increasing civil strife:

> 'An advocate of actions and measures, which on the face of them, were designed to serve the purpose of achieving the maximum degree of publicity, and at the least to render likely a confrontation between police and demonstrators which could readily develop into violent disorder. He was

particularly active in the organization of "Free Derry" and in the operation of its short-lived radio broadcasts. We regard him and his aims and activities as playing an important part in the agitations which are associated with the disorders of October (1968) onwards.'[4]

Into the already highly charged and emotional atmosphere of Northern Ireland another force, openly speaking of the need not for reform but for revolution, was thus introduced in addition to the IRA. In the first days of 1969 this new force was instrumental in launching a venture which caused a disastrous deterioration in the situation—the march it organized from Belfast to Londonderry, which ran into violent and organized Protestant opposition, especially the famous ambush at Burntollet Bridge. The decision to march was taken after the then Prime Minister of Northern Ireland, Captain Terence O'Neill, had announced the Unionist Government's reform policy, and People's Democracy immediately announced that it found this completely unacceptable, despite the fact that the Civil Rights leadership was trying to cool down public opinion in order to give the programme a chance. The result that this march produced is best illustrated by a further quotation from the Cameron Report:

'For moderates this march had a disastrous effect. It polarized the extreme elements in the communities in each place it entered. It lost sympathy for the Civil Rights movement and led to serious rioting in Maghera and Londonderry. It divided the Civil Rights movement and weakened the Derry Citizens Action Committee. We are driven to think that the leaders must have intended that their venture would weaken the moderate reforming forces in Northern Ireland. We think that their object was to increase tension, so that in the process a more radical programme could be realized.'

At the same time PD was making vigorous efforts to extend its influence inside the Civil Rights movement, which it did partly by promoting the formation of a large number of Civil Rights branches composed of members sympathetic to PD policies, who each had the right to send representatives to the Civil Rights policy-making council.

4 *Disturbances in Northern Ireland*, CMD 532 (1969), paragraph 201

In March 1969, Miss Betty Sinclair, the first chairman of Civil Rights, alarmed at PD's efforts to gain control and to force the pace, resigned. Although an admitted Communist, she had always stood out against the use of violence and ultra-militant methods. Her resignation was accompanied by that of three other leading members. Shortly afterwards the new chairman, Frank Gogarty, caused consternation amongst remaining moderates when he announced that the movement had surrendered its autonomy and right of independent action in the interests of 'coordinated policy'. Taking this to be a surrender to PD pressure, John McAnery, Civil Rights Association Secretary, thereupon also resigned.

The changing nature of the Civil Rights movement which was now so clearly becoming evident also began to worry those hitherto sympathetic outside its ranks. One who clearly expressed this growing concern was an American lawyer who early in 1969 had collected £450 in his own country to aid the Civil Rights Association's campaign. He flew to Ulster with the aim of presenting a cheque for this amount to a rally being organized by the Association in Lurgan. He was so disturbed, however, at the repeated chanting of slogans by many of those present in praise of Mao Tse-tung and Ho Chi Minh that he left in indignation; saying that he was so shocked that he was not now prepared to give the movement a cent of the money he had taken so much trouble to raise.

Members of People's Democracy were active in organizing the defences of the Bogside in Londonderry during the months that led up to the culminating clash on the day of the Apprentice Boys' March on 13 August, the clash that was to spark off widespread disturbances throughout almost the entire province. These months were marked by growing efforts by Civil Rights supporters, aided, or sometimes embarrassed by, hooligan and extremist elements to transform the Bogside and adjacent districts into what have come to be known as 'no-go areas'. Although at first the emphasis was on defence against attack by militant Protestants, it also very soon came to embrace the barring of the entry of members of the security forces and the general defying of authority.

These preparations for defence came to be largely under the charge of a new organization, the Derry Citizens Defence

Association, with a much more militant stance than any that had preceded it in the area. Of its original eight-man committee seven members were also members of the illegal James Connolly Republican Club, although later it drew in additional members from a wider spectrum. This committee proceeded to form street committees, each under its own chairman. The sites of barricades were decided upon, and although the use of firearms was barred members were encouraged to prepare to defend themselves with 'sticks, stones, and the good old petrol bomb'.[5] Committee leaders did nothing to disabuse a growing impression amongst residents of the Bogside that the police force was a partisan one opposed to the Catholic Community.

Although the Scarman Report found no evidence of any plot to bring about the rioting which broke out in Londonderry on 11 August and so rapidly spread, it did find that:

> 'Although there was no conspiracy in the sense in which that term is normally used (for it is not possible to identify any group or groups of persons deliberately planning the riots of 1969) yet it would be the height of naïvety to deny that the teenage hooligans, who almost invariably threw the first stones, were manipulated and encouraged by persons seeking to discredit the Government. While accepting that the major riots that occurred in Londonderry, Belfast, Armagh and Dungannon were not deliberately planned, we are satisfied that, once the disturbances started, they were continued by an element that also found expression in bodies more or less loosely organized, such as the People's Democracy, and the various local defence associations, and in associating themselves with bodies such as NICRA and the several action committees. The public impact of the activities of this element was tremendously enhanced by the coverage given by the mass media of communication.'[6]

The rapid spreading of the riots after their outbreak in Londonderry was certainly no mere case of spontaneous com-

[5] *Violence and Civil Disturbances in Northern Ireland in 1969.* CMD 566 (1969), paragraph 10.12
[6] Ibid., paragraph 2.2

bustion. On the evening of 12 August, when the Londonderry riots were at their height, Mr Gogarty, chairman of the Civil Rights Association, came under severe pressure from a number of people, including Bernadette Devlin, Eamonn McCann and the chairman of the Derry Citizens Defence Committee, to take the heat off the Bogside by organizing a number of diversionary demonstrations elsewhere in the Province which would distract the attention of the already hard-pressed police.

Despite the fact that a ban on public demonstrations was imposed by the Government that night, the Civil Rights Executive, whose membership now included several staunch republicans and whose links extended to several leading IRA figures, met the following morning and decided to ask their branches to stand by to mount diversionary demonstrations as requested; and at the same time decided to inform the Minister for Home Affairs that these would be set in motion unless the police were withdrawn from the Bogside forthwith. The demonstrations were subsequently launched and led to outbreaks of violence in a number of centres. It was afterwards found that:

> 'The association did not advocate violence but it encouraged a course of action which might well, as in the event it did, offer to others less well-controlled the opportunity that was seized in many centres, and most dramatically in Belfast itself.'[7]

In fact the Civil Rights Executive had excluded Belfast from the areas in which it planned diversionary operations through fear of causing major communal disturbances; but a curious and still unexplained incident ensured that the call for support for the defenders of the Bogside found its way to the capital of the Province despite this.

In the early evening of 13 August, a policeman on duty near the large council blocks known as Unity Flats in West Belfast heard and saw a loudspeaker mounted on a white Cortina car being used to call people to a meeting to be held in a nearby area, and appealing for support for the fighters of the Bogside. The meeting was subsequently held, considerably increasing tension; it played an important part in starting the train of events which

[7] *Violence and Civil Disturbances in Northern Ireland in 1969.* CMD 566 (1969), paragraph 2.2

127

led to the wave of savage rioting in Belfast in the following days, which was to cause such immense suffering and damage, and which within three days was to cause the intervention of the British Army in the city for the first time.

Later enquiries revealed that the white Cortina had on the evening in question been lent by its owner to a man he claimed not to know for a purpose he did not know, but which he had believed to be that of 'refugee relief'. Who organized and spoke at the meeting remains undetermined as reports vary in their descriptions of those responsible from those of students and young Civil Rights supporters to those of well-known personalities who had appeared on television.

The nature of People's Democracy had been meanwhile undergoing a change, much of the less extreme student support it had at first attracted dropped away, and it began to reveal itself as a small but dedicated revolutionary group composed largely of convinced Trotskyists and anarchists, with the influence of the former more and more dominant. Ties with the International Socialists increased, and Bernadette Devlin became a frequent contributor to its paper *Socialist Worker*. In the autumn of 1969 a leading PD member stated that most of the founder members of the movement and those then prominent in it regarded themselves as being International Socialists.

With the slackening of the rioting of 1969 PD began to try to implement its plans for building a united-revolutionary front between Catholic and Protestant workers by concentrating upon social campaigns (such as one against fare increases on Belfast public transport), and upon the publication of a paper, *The Free Citizen*. Whilst the opening of the IRA campaign of terrorism at the beginning of 1970 tended to push both the People's Democracy and the Civil Rights Association into the background, militant PD activity was again stepped up after the introduction of internment in August 1971. The campaign to build a common front between Catholic and Protestant workers had produced few results, and it was decided to again concentrate activity upon Catholic areas. PD members have been active in encouraging various forms of civil resistance in such areas and have been attempting to build links between the various defence and resistance committees, both within individual towns and across the country. PD has cooperated from time to time with both the Official and Provisional IRA.

A new development made itself manifest early in 1972 with the setting up of the Northern Resistance Movement, in which Michael Farrell took a leading part. This seemed to represent a coming together of People's Democracy and the Provisional IRA; the idea was that PD should provide the brains of the new grouping whilst the Provisionals provided the brawn. This development occurred at much the same time as reports first began to circulate about Trotskyists of the IV International and the Provisionals, but the scheme ran into some opposition from purely nationalist elements in the Provisionals, and its final outcome appeared uncertain.

THE NEW IRA

The birth of the new Marxist-orientated IRA after the failure of the border campaign was largely due to the efforts of its present Chief of Staff, Cathal Goulding, and a small group of Marxist intellectuals; chief amongst whom was Dr Roy Johnston, centred round the Wolfe Tone Society in Trinity College, Dublin. The group had been much influenced by Desmond Greaves of the Communist Party of Great Britain, and by members of a long-established Communist front, the Connolly Association.

Goulding was later to explain that the main problem facing the IRA High Command at this time was quite simply how could they get people to support them, in the light of their failure to do so during the border campaign. In the recent past the object of the IRA had been to fight to rid Ireland of British rule and connections, and little else. What was now lacking was any sort of political programme that could persuade people that once this had been accomplished they would be individually better off.

The policy that was decided upon was the typical Marxist one of trying to identify the IRA and its political wing, the Sinn Fein, with demands for better pay, better housing, education and similar domestic topics, so that people would become involved in a campaign of making revolutionary social demands which the existing system could not possibly fulfil.

Accordingly, from 1964 onwards the IRA and Sinn Fein

embarked upon a thoroughgoing campaign of social and political agitation in the Irish Republic along these lines. Much activity centred on agitation over housing problems and trade union activity. For publicity purposes tactics such as 'fish-ins'—organized illegal fishing on private river beats—and propaganda campaigns over the preservation of Georgian buildings in Dublin were followed.

By the beginning of 1965 the campaign was beginning to cause some alarm to the Dublin Government. Confirming the existence of the new alliance between the IRA and Communism, Brian Lenihan, then Minister of Justice, said:

'Although small in membership the Communist Front and its allies have succeeded in recent months by insidious propaganda in becoming front-page news in the daily newspapers.

'They have organized marches and near riots, which have caused considerable disruption of traffic and trouble to the Gardai, the courts and the public.'[8]

The Minister also stated that it was known that the previous year a leading Communist had been accepted as a member of the IRA and had been given charge of its propaganda machine.

The new policies of the IRA marked an innovation in more than one way, for increasingly the emphasis was laid upon the importance of political work first and armed action later, whereas the whole emphasis previously had been on preparations for armed action only. Moreover, the question of the abolition of the border now became secondary to the establishment of 'socialism' in the whole of Ireland.

In the spring of 1965 Mr Lenihan announced that a plan for the subversion of both the existing Irish Governments, Northern and Southern, and the unification of the country in the form of a 32-county 'Socialist Workers Republic' had been found in the possession of a leading member of an 'illegal organization' and would be put before the senate. A similar plan of apparently later date came into the hands of the Royal Ulster Constabulary Special Branch, and was published as an appendix to the report of the Scarman Tribunal. Although IRA sources have claimed the plan was never anything more than a discussion document, it does

[8] *Belfast Telegraph*, 3 January, 1965

give practical indication of the new thinking of IRA leaders at the end of the 1960s, and moreover some of the tactics and methods of organization suggested do seem to have been put into practice in Ulster later.

After stressing the importance of work amongst trade unionists so as to make them 'more revolutionary', the plan lays great importance on the building up of an effective propaganda organization:

'Due to the failure of our own organizational structure to cope with the changed environment and strategy, the organizational form whereby agitational work has been carried out has been the "ad-hoc" Committee. This form of organization suffers from defects; lack of discipline and lack of coordination of effort being the principal ones.

'Formal committees should be set up to cover various fields and to work short term limited objectives . . .

'There should be formal committees dealing with housing questions, Free Trade, cooperativism, etc. These committees will work with other radical-minded groups such as the Labour Party people, Trade Union people, etc. These committees are to have such an organizational structure to enable them to mobilize the mass of the membership of the Movement in any agitation.'[9]

The syllabus for the training of IRA recruits was also to be re-drafted so as to explain that in future the role of armed action would be to back up political action 'legally initiated'. In future the political organization of the movement would be based on both local and factory branches (on classic Communist Party lines). There were also to be special groups such as Tenants' Associations, youth groups, cooperative and credit union groups etc. The aim of these groups was to be 'dynamos generating local and specialized Republican leadership in all areas of the peoples' needs'. They were also to act as 'a training ground for revolutionary government'.

In another important paragraph it was emphasized that the new constitution of the movement should:

'. . . be drafted in such a way as to allow for affiliation of

[9] Appendix V (B), *Violence and Civil Disturbances in Northern Ireland in 1969*, paragraph 2

friendly organizations, giving the possibility of having a vast and diversified movement under the Republican umbrella. Affiliations to be accepted from Trade Unions, Felons Clubs, co-operatives, Wolfe Tone Societies and all such bodies with objectives that do not conflict with the objectives of the Movement. Affiliations to be possible both regionally, locally and nationally (consult with heads of such groups) to make objectives part of national objective.'[10]

Elections were to be contested for both the Northern and Southern Parliaments, but not until suitable candidates had been sufficiently prepared so as to give a good account of themselves.

On the military side the plan suggested an 'anti-agent' campaign; it was explained that this would mean the killing of not only Special Branch policemen but also ordinary policemen who acted as agents against the IRA. It was suggested that an immediate start should be made on this campaign, part of the object of which was to harden members of the organization and to 'get our people psychologically prepared for future killing'. Another suggestion was for 'large stunt-type operations'; the object of these being described as being of a purely 'killing nature' aimed at causing as many fatal casualties to the British Army as possible.

The plan advocated that, as far as the operations in Northern Ireland were concerned:

'Due to the limited area of operation, the density and hostility of population, the vast array of police and other paramilitary and military forces under the control of the enemy, we believe that classic guerrilla-type operations cannot be successful. Here we must learn from the Cypriots and engage in terror tactics only.'[11]

The operational organization envisaged was to be based upon a cell system with not more than four members in each cell. It was suggested that four such units should be active in each postal district in Belfast, each district having its own leader. Cells should be organized in factories, other places of employment, and clubs where those involved came together naturally in the course of their normal daily activities.

[10] Appendix V (B), *Violence and Civil Disturbances in Northern Ireland in 1969*, p. 47
[11] Ibid., p. 50

Despite this sort of contingency planning there would seem to be no doubt that the outbreak of the first violent clashes between members of the two communities in Ulster and between demonstrators and the police in 1968 took the IRA badly by surprise, and found it in the midst of major reorganization and reappraisal and quite unready for action from a military aspect. This unreadiness remained a major brake on its effective intervention even as the troubles escalated through 1969, although IRA efforts to manipulate the Civil Rights movement noticeably increased and its hand was evident behind the formation of many of the 'Citizens Defence Committees' that sprang up in Belfast, Londonderry, and such centres as Newry and Lurgan. A Royal Ulster Constabulary Special Branch Report of August 1969 said of these organizations:

'These local bodies, as stated, were all Republican and IRA dominated. Their outward and publicly announced policies were "peaceful" and for the "protection" of local communities. We now know, to our cost, *vide* Derry, that under this cloak of peace they were in fact preparing for war.'

It does not seem, however, that it was until about mid-summer that Cathal Goulding started to seriously look round for sources of arms with which to equip a new military campaign. By the end of August he was coming under increasing pressure and criticism because of the IRA's inability to defend Catholic areas against the mob attacks of the Protestant backlash in Belfast. Meanwhile certain events had already been in train for some months behind the scenes with the greatest importance for the future.

THE EMERGENCE OF THE PROVISIONALS

The Goulding group's new policies and organizational reforms had always been unpopular with some of the old-timers in the ranks of the IRA, in some cases because of the drift towards socialism, but perhaps more evidently because of the emphasis on the need for political action and the relegation of armed action to second place. Criticism increased amongst this element, particularly amongst leading members of it in Belfast, as Goulding's inability or unwillingness to organize more forceful intervention in the developing situation in the North became more apparent.

133

In February 1970 contacts were first made independently of IRA Headquarters in Dublin between a leading member of the IRA in Londonderry and a representative of certain political and business circles in the Irish Republic. These contacts were to lead to somewhat involved and tortuous negotiations[12] in which was involved, amongst others, the former Irish Army Intelligence Officer who was later to figure in the Dublin arms-smuggling trial, Captain James Kelly; one of the most important events was a meeting held in a Belfast social club at the end of August.

The meeting was attended by most leading members of the IRA in Northern Ireland and a party from the South, including a Dublin politician and Captain Kelly. The meeting was told that Sean MacStiofan, then the IRA's Headquarters Director of Intelligence, was in favour of more radical action and of a break with the Dublin command. It was thereupon agreed that plans should be laid for the overthrowing of the IRA Command in Belfast, which was known to be loyal to Goulding; and for the establishment of a separate Belfast Command with its own policies.

This meeting was soon followed by another, this time in the little village of Moville in Donegal. At this meeting the representative of the Dublin political and business group clearly showed its hand. The group, he said, would undertake to raise £200,000 for the purchase of arms and other requirements, if the IRA for its part undertook to stop all political activity in the Republic and to establish an independent Belfast Headquarters which would be responsible for managing a military campaign in the six counties of the North.

The closing months of 1969 were marked by a coming together of those who were to become leaders of the Provisionals in preparations to constitute a force to begin an armed struggle. There were not many possible recruits to choose from as the entire IRA organization in Belfast at that time probably only consisted of about eighty active members. Still, the leaders of the embryo organization were encouraged when support was received from the officers of nine out of the eleven IRA companies in the city. The incipient split in the movement came when the anti-Gould-

[12] Described in detail by The *Sunday Times* Insight Team in *Ulster*, André Deutsch (London, 1972)

ing faction, headed by MacStiofan, walked out of the annual IRA conference in Dublin at the end of November, with their announcement of the establishment of the 'Provisional Army Council', dedicated to support 'the 32-county Irish Republic proclaimed at Easter 1916 . . . overthrown by force of arms in 1922 and suppressed to this day'. A parallel split occurring in the Sinn Fein conference held in January 1970.

Despite the fact that funds were promised by the Dublin business and political group, at the start of their existence the Provisionals found themselves woefully short of arms, as all the quartermasters of the Belfast area who had charge of such weapons as the IRA had in the city remained loyal to Goulding's Dublin Headquarters and its supporters of the 'Official' IRA, as it was now to become known. A windfall came their way, however, when IRA units in three counties south of the border switched their allegiance to the Provisionals and sent their arms, including thirty Thompson submachine guns. Some money from the South also reached them.

Early in 1970 members of the Provisionals, together with some members of local defence committees, went over the border to train in various parts of the Republic and undertook an intensive study of the tactics of past guerrilla campaigns. Within quite a short time the Provisionals were the dominating influence in the Belfast IRA organization, the officials being left with only two districts as undisputed bases of their own, the Falls and the Turf Lodge areas. Relations between the army and the Catholic population on the whole remained good, but it is thought that the Provisionals deliberately set out to try to spoil these.

The spring and early summer saw the first serious clashes between Catholic crowds and the Army, mainly in the Ballymurphy area, which became one of the Provisionals' main strongholds. On 1 July members of the Officials opened fire on the Army during an arms search in the Falls. Shooting incidents thereafter progressively increased, although it was not until February of the following year that the first fatal army casualty occurred, during a search for leading members of the Provisionals. The following morning the then Prime Minister of Ulster announced on television: 'Northern Ireland is at war with the Irish Republican Army Provos.'

Although the split between the Provisionals and the Officials is often portrayed as being due essentially to the Marxist nature of the latter and the 'anti-red' nationalism of the former, this would seem to be an over-simplification, and in fact the differences between the two were probably due as much to fundamental disagreement over tactics as over strategy or political philosophy.

In such literature as they have produced defining their political aims, the views of the Provisionals regarding the shape of the new Ireland, which it hoped the present struggle will produce, do not seem to differ very greatly from those of the Officials. Like the Officials they proclaim their belief in building a Socialist Workers Republic, and in one policy document have explained that in such a state finance, insurance and all key industries must be state-controlled, and that the state must also be the principal agent of major development in both industry and agriculture. Private enterprise would be allowed no part in key industries, with the main instrument of development apart from the state being co-operatives.

It is probable that the main reason for the split between the two movements was that the Provisionals felt the time for armed action had arrived, whilst the Officials still felt the emphasis should be on political work.

It would seem that whilst some Provisionals base their opposition to the political line of the Officials on their own anti-Marxist nationalism, another, and perhaps predominant, faction does so from the point of view of the revolutionary left's dislike of orthodox Communism. It was presumably this faction which was responsible for allegedly making contacts with Trotskyists of the IV International early in 1972. The IV International has a section in Dublin and a small group of supporters in Belfast. The Dublin section was formed by the late Peter Graham, in 1971, who was a leading member of the IV International's British affiliate, the International Marxist Group, in which Gerry Lawless, formerly a member of the IRA and active in early Civil Rights activities in Ulster, is also prominent. Lawless at present heads the Irish Solidarity Campaign in Britain. The IV International has adopted the slogan 'Victory to the IRA' and has been organizing valuable propaganda support on an international scale.

136

THE BOMBING CAMPAIGN

The Provisional IRA's bombing campaign commenced with attacks on a fairly restricted list of targets, and with considerable effort made to minimize the risk of casualties. In a matter of months, however, the point had been reached where all such precautions and restrictions had almost completely disappeared, and many explosions were accompanied by considerable casualties. In September 1971, the Provisionals' Chief of Staff, Sean MacStiofan, asked if he considered the killing and maiming of civilians mattered, replied frankly that he did not think it did. Everything had become 'fair game', he said, and it was now the Provisional plan to make everyone concerned pay dear 'and very dear' for the continued presence of British troops in the province.

By October the same year between forty and fifty factories had been damaged by bombs; whilst seventy public houses, another favourite target, had been destroyed since 1969. The bombing campaign reached a peak that month, in which no less than 279 explosions occurred. More than £1 million worth of damage was done and the jobs of some 500 people were lost as the result of the bombing of one factory near the centre of Belfast in December. The weeks immediately before Christmas saw an intensification of the bombing campaign in a deliberate attempt to wreck the centre of the city and cause as much disruption as possible during the pre-Christmas shopping rush. The widely varying nature of the targets chosen by the Provisionals is well illustrated by a list of premises attacked in Belfast on the one day of 21 December. These included a co-operative store, a café, an antiques shop, an insurance office, a furniture shop, a television office, a clothing factory, an hotel, and one of the city's railway stations.

The Provisionals have made very few attacks on targets that could in any way be considered of a military nature, and have in fact stated that it is not their policy to go in for any 'suicide mission' attacks on well-guarded buildings, but instead to concentrate upon 'soft targets' of the type indicated. Their tactics have been proclaimed as a 'war of attrition', apparently designed to bring about a state of psychological exhaustion amongst their opponents by the use of almost any means. Any bomb successfully planted in the centre of a town 'knocks the morale of the British Army', one of their spokesmen announced.

It seems clear that the great majority of attacks have been aimed principally at hitting the headlines of the press and other news media, thus creating a growing sense of insecurity and giving the impression to the outside world that the province is ungovernable under its present system of administration. One British Army expert has said that the amount of explosives used in this campaign 'just blacks out Aden or Cyprus into the shade'. There were a total of 750 explosions during the first ten months of 1971; the army disarmed a further 400 bombs during the same period. And whereas in most previous terrorist campaigns bombs have tended to contain about 1 lb. of explosives, bombs containing 25 lb. or more, capable of wrecking whole buildings and creating extensive damage over a wide area, have not been uncommon in Ulster.

Early in 1972 a major disaster was only narrowly averted when army experts succeeded in disarming a bomb which had been attached to a 3,500-gallon petrol tanker, which had been hijacked in Belfast and left in the centre of the nearby town of Lisburn. An army officer said that had an explosion occurred a large area of the town would have certainly been destroyed. Sophisticated anti-handling devices have often been attached to bombs, although this has become less common as arrests by security forces have made inroads into the ranks of the Provisionals' expert bomb-makers. One Provisional detained in the Anderstown area claimed himself to have been responsible for the planting of fifty-nine bombs. It would appear, however, that as Provisional casualties have risen the actual planting of bombs has frequently been done by teenagers, not themselves members of the IRA, who have been approached in cafés or clubs by members of the Provisionals, and bribed, flattered or intimidated into 'doing a job for Ireland'.

The mounting concern of the Provisionals to limit all possible risk to members engaged in the bombing campaign led to new tactics early in 1972. Instead of bombs being placed in buildings, they were now more usually left in stolen cars or lorries parked at strategic spots in chosen streets. This had the added advantage, from the terrorists' point of view, of whole streets having to be cleared instead of just one building when warnings were given, thus further disrupting normal life; and the difficulty of clearing busy streets in the very short warning period usually allowed meant the number of casualties caused by the bombing campaign were sharply increased.

On some occasions no warning at all has been given before bombs in cars or commercial vehicles have exploded in crowded shopping areas. In one incident early in January 1972, a beer and spirits lorry was hijacked by gunmen in the Lower Falls district of Belfast. It was driven to a street near the city centre, which was at its height of the New Year sales and crowded with shoppers, and abandoned. Shortly after midday a bomb on the vehicle exploded without any warning, and over sixty people were injured. On one or two occasions there seems to have been a deliberate intent to cause the maximum number of casualties possible by giving misleading warnings. One case in point was the explosion in Donegal Street, Belfast, in which six people were killed and 152 injured in March 1972. A warning was given that a bomb had been left in a car in an adjoining street. This was cleared, many of those in it flocked into Donegal Street seeking safety; in fact the car with the bomb was in Donegal Street, and exploded with the maximum effect just when the street was abnormally crowded.

The full effect of this totally indiscriminate form of terrorism, used apparently purely to destroy morale and create a sense of panic, has been vividly portrayed in an on-the-spot description by a young British soldier on patrol in Belfast at the time of one explosion:

'We had been cruising around the Sandy Row area when a bomb warning came over the radio. Immediately the Land Rover accelerated. With lights on and a hand on the horn, the driver took us at high speed to a street where a bomb was reported. At each end of the street was a large crowd, so our first job was to disperse these people, get them as far away as possible. This we did in a few minutes ... After about ten minutes some Paras came over to help us find the bomb which was said to be in a yellow car. We couldn't find a yellow car, let alone a parcel or box. So we searched other cars, obviously not opening them, but just walking up and down the street looking in through car windows. Then from down the bottom of the street we heard a big blast. At that moment we ran to the Rovers, which were already moving and jumped on. We were down at the bomb site only a few seconds later, because it was only about 200 yards from where we were searching the cars. Before we stopped I could see confusion everywhere.

'As we jumped out to go inside, I saw a woman lying on the pavement. There were several people round her, so I carried on. As I passed her all that I could see of her face was red. Also the front of her coat—blood-red. There were people panicking everywhere. Young girls in hysterics and others just walking about the rubble at the entrance of the Europa Hotel, in a daze. All round the front were small metal road barriers. We had to jump over these to get within twenty yards of the building. All over the floor at this point was broken glass. It seemed as if it were several inches deep and it was still falling from the higher floors of the building.

'Once inside, the first person I saw was a man walking about in front of me, with his hand on the back of his neck. Blood was oozing out between his fingers. I took his hand away and what I saw I cannot put into words, just that a big chunk of glass must have hit him. I started to put my field dressing on him and a doctor came up to help. So I left him and went on. It was then that it dawned on me—the mess of the place inside—doors were blown out, windows shattered and, as outside, broken glass all over the floors. The next person I saw was a lad of about 17 years, leaning against a wall. I asked him where he was injured; he said his back. I lifted his jumper up a bit but it was sticking to him. Then a nurse came up, she took out some scissors and we cut away his jumper which revealed his blood-red shirt. We cut that away, which left his back. He had a large cut across his back, it was bleeding badly. We patched him up, then I heard a scream behind me. I turned round and there was this girl coming towards me. Her hand was covered in blood. She grabbed me with the good hand and put the other round me. She was shouting something like "Get me out of here, for God's sake, get me out". I took her into what used to be the coffee bar and started to clean her hand up. She had a ring on one of her fingers and something had hit her hand because the ring was nearly squeezed shut. I cleaned her up as much as I could, while I was doing this I talked to her.

'Then she started to smile between sobs, then she started to laugh and said that her boyfriend had just been posted to Hong Kong the day before. She kept on saying it. And by the look of her face she was glad that he had missed this and was safe. Then I took her outside to wait for an ambulance.

'We were then pulled out and told to go and watch a funeral pass across a crossroad. There was no trouble and it was over in a few minutes. So we then carried out the rest of our patrol. Several times we were asked "How many were killed in the blast?" (not—"Was there anyone killed?" but "How many?"). Luckily, nobody was killed but 70 people were reported injured.'

Despite some appalling incidents causing heavy casualties such as the one described above, the explosion in Donegal Street and the explosion in the Abercorn Restaurant in Belfast in late March which killed two and wounded 136, the overall number of bombing incidents continued to fall during the early months of 1972, owing to the increased successes of the security forces; but then it climbed sharply again immediately after the introduction of direct rule until at one time in mid-April a bomb was exploding somewhere in the Province on an average of one an hour.

The indiscriminate nature of the bombing campaign has ensured that many Catholics as well as Protestants have suffered physical injury as well as damage to property. But some attacks on public houses and other premises in wholly Protestant areas do seem to have been deliberately aimed at provoking a backlash and setting the two communities at each other's throats, tactics of much the same type as those employed by the terrorists of the FLN in Algeria.

The Official IRA has several times denounced this side of the Provisionals' bombing campaign as being counter-productive and militating against any chance of building a common revolutionary front of Catholic and Protestant workers. The Officials, however, retain the right to carry out bombing attacks on military targets,

and what are described as 'retaliatory bombings' against individuals or groups who have particularly opposed their policies, or
such targets as 'bars used by Special Branch men'. They have in
fact been responsible for a number of bomb attacks upon property
in Ulster, notably that upon the home of Senator Barnhill in
Strabane, in the course of which he was murdered, and upon the
Paratroop barracks in Aldershot which resulted in the death of
five people and injuries to seventeen more.

THE GUNMEN

The basic operational unit of the Provisional IRA is the so-
called 'active service unit', usually five- to eight-man cells allowed
a considerable measure of autonomy and making great use of
stolen motor transport to provide mobility. Engagements with the
army usually take the form of brief sniping episodes, with cars
at the ready for a quick getaway. Gunmen of the Official IRA
claim to act according to a more defensively designed programme
than that of the Provisionals, but in effect use much the same
tactics, if on a more limited scale.

In April 1972 it was estimated that there were probably no
more than a total of 300 gunmen of both wings of the IRA
active in Ulster (though these were assisted by a very much
larger number of auxiliaries and supporters of various kinds). Of
these about 200 were thought to be based in the Bogside and
Creggan areas of Londonderry and about 100 in Belfast. It was
believed that a number of activists had recently returned from
sanctuary in the Irish Republic in the hope that the introduction
of direct rule would mean a less rigorous enforcement of security
measures.

Although few in numbers IRA gunmen have managed to sus-
tain a high level of activity over short periods of time. In one
period of intense activity during the autumn of 1971 British
Army units came under fire fifty-four times in three days, on
seventeen of these occasions the fire being from automatic
weapons. In the first ten months of that year army units were
fired upon 1,355 times. A spate of incidents involving IRA gunmen and the security forces occurred in April 1972. In one day
that month there were fifty-six shooting incidents around the
area of Divis Flats in Belfast alone, whilst no less than 1,240

rounds were fired at the security forces during the seventy-two-hour period that ended on the early morning of 18 April. By 21 April there had been 200 shooting incidents in the province in the preceding five days. Shooting incidents between IRA snipers in the Bogside and army posts surrounding the area became almost daily and nightly events during the latter part of 1971 and early 1972, whilst elsewhere army patrols were repeatedly fired on from across the border.

Fire has often been opened by the IRA with little or no regard for the safety of nearby civilians, and the casualties, like those in bomb explosions, have caused little concern to the IRA High Command. The death of a 17-month-old child in Belfast from a bullet fired by a Provisional sniper was dismissed by the Provisional's Chief of Staff, Rory O'Brady, as 'one of the hazards of urban guerrilla warfare'.

On some occasions it would seem that there have been deliberate attempts to force the army into returning fire in such a way that civilian casualties would be likely to obtain propaganda advantage. In one such case, it appeared that gunmen deliberately fired in the direction of a small car crammed with five people, including three young children. Gangs of stone-throwing youths have often been used to screen snipers and to draw troops who have been trying to quell disturbances into their field of fire.

By the end of 1971 nearly sixty British soldiers had been killed, mainly as a result of sniper fire. The IRA casualties were not known in detail as wounded gunmen or other dead bodies seldom fall into the hands of the security forces, but evidence of a heavy toll has been apparent. As losses have increased, the IRA have been making increasing use of members of its Youth Movement, the Fiana Na Fail, to replenish the ranks of its gunmen. In one incident two boys, one of them armed with a tommy gun, opened fire on an army patrol from a Belfast street corner in daylight. One local Provisional commander in Belfast thought to have been responsible for several deaths is only 15 years old.

Cases have also occurred in which women have opened fire on security forces, and it is thought that they have also been used to a considerable extent for bomb planting.

Gunmen of both the Officials and Provisionals have received training, military and political, in considerable numbers in special camps scattered throughout the Irish Republic. In the summer of 1971 two correspondents of a British Sunday newspaper were allowed to visit one such camp. This was based upon three white-washed cottages near the coast at Mornington, Drogheda, and was managed by the part of Sinn Fein attached to the Official IRA. The reporters saw IRA students from Belfast undergoing instruction in a classroom, at the top of which was a blackboard bearing the slogan for the week. It read:

'To make a revolution you need revolutionaries. Conscious, informed, and experienced revolutionaries make successful revolutions.'

They were told that although military training did not take place in that particular camp, guerrilla warfare training courses were 'easily arranged' in other parts of the country; and that the aim of the political training being imparted at this particular camp was to enable students to demonstrate to both Catholics and Protestants that 'there was a need for a revolution in Ireland'.

INTIMIDATION AND PROPAGANDA

Intimidation by both wings of the IRA, mainly directed at the Catholic population, the sea in which it hopes to swim, has been a constant feature of the campaign from the outset. Actual or suspected informers have been tied to lamp posts and slashed with razors; shot through both elbows or knees; repeatedly burnt with red-hot pokers; subjected to electric shock tortures; and not infrequently killed. IRA 'kangaroo courts' often closely interrogate persons known to have been questioned by the Army or Police in order to try to ascertain if they have given any information. The atmosphere of fear engendered by the use of such methods can be appreciated from the fact that a comparatively unimportant IRA suspect pleaded when brought in for questioning by the Special Branch not to be released—he feared for his life if he was.

In another case, a man was found lying in a central Belfast car park with both his legs broken as the result of a car being driven back and forth over him. However, he refused to give any information about his attackers beyond saying that he had written down their three names and put the paper away in a sealed envelope which the police might find if he was killed, but apart from that he was not prepared to help in any way. The prevalence of intimidation has made it also extremely difficult to find witnesses willing to come forward to give evidence in Crown prosecution cases, and hence almost impossible to fulfil the often-repeated demand that internees should be put on trial. One witness who did volunteer to come forward was a 40-year-old bus driver in Belfast; before the case could be heard he was shot in his own home by terrorists in front of his 82-year-old mother-in-law.

Concerted attempts have also been made to discourage recruiting for the Ulster Defence Regiment and the Police by the ruthless shooting of members of both forces. In the case of members of the Ulster Defence Regiment this has usually meant attacks upon members when off duty and unarmed. Catholic members of the regiment are particular targets. One such member was sitting at home in Belfast watching television, when a masked gunman rushed in and shot him dead in front of his wife and four children. His eldest daughter, aged 10, was also hit and wounded by a bullet. In another case a bus driver member of the UDR was pulled off his bus and shortly afterwards found shot with his hands tied behind him. In yet another instance a UDR corporal was kidnapped by terrorists from the border whilst off duty and a few days later his body was found lying on farm land on the frontier. Six 'claymore' mines, each capable of destroying an armoured car, had been put in the area surrounding it, and the body itself was booby-trapped by being attached to a 200 lb. bomb.

In some Catholic areas intimidation has been used to enforce participation in the rent strike organized by the Civil Rights Association and other committees, and supported by the IRA. One leaflet distributed in the Ballymurphy area of Belfast said that anyone who did not cooperate fully and 'stand solid' with the strikers must accept the consequences. Another circulating in the Anderstown area contained a space for householders' signatures below a statement of support for the strike, and the warning 'failure to sign will mean that you will not be entitled to the protection which your signature would give'.

From the earliest days of its existence the IRA has known full well the immense importance of propaganda, not only in

enrolling the support of the population at home but also in in-
fluencing public opinion abroad. Its skills in this art have now
been further increased by its recent study of Marxist techniques.
In the mid-1960s, at the suggestion of Dr Roy Johnston, it
introduced Education Officers into the establishment of its units.
These officers, who now are present down to company level in
the IRA structure, have responsibility both for the political education of members of the IRA itself and for directing local propaganda activities directed at the public and the news media.

A leading member of the Official IRA, Malachy McGurran,
has explained the way in which political and military training is
now closely intertwined in the instruction given to recruits to his
wing of the movement. He has said that recruits are told:

'You must understand the politics that motivate the movement. We are not going to give a man a gun just to have
a crack at the British Army. We give a volunteer a weapon,
we explain to him how it works, how it is loaded, how it
fires, how to aim it, how to strip it, how to clean it. Then
we explain our policies, what we want and how to get it.
These two, the weapon and the politics, must be merged
together. Without the politics, the rifle, the revolver and the
machine gun are all useless. But without the weapon, the
politics are sterile . . .'[13]

McGurran has also said that he thinks that it is 'incredibly
important to involve the English working class in our struggle':

'You have only got to think of the French people demanding the withdrawal of their troops from Algeria, and the
same with the Americans in Vietnam, and then you realise
the importance of the English working class. But they must
realise they are helping us for class reasons, not because
of some nationalistic notions. They must do it, because
it will help them in the long run to advance their own
socialism, not just the quasi-socialism of Harold Wilson.
Over here, all we can do is set the example, as Cuba set
the example for Latin America.'[13]

From the troubles that led up to the creation of the Irish
Republic onwards, a great deal of IRA propaganda has been
concentrated upon the manufacture of atrocity stories regarding

[13] 7 *Days*, 8 March 1972

the behaviour of the security forces opposing them, and this has again occupied much of the attention of the IRA's propaganda machine during the present campaign. A favourite allegation has been that of misbehaviour by troops during searches. On several occasions lurid stories have appeared in the press about such alleged misconduct, only for residents in areas where it is supposed to have taken place to say later that they knew nothing of the incident or that the reports have been grossly exaggerated.

In one typical such incident a report appeared in the *Irish News* that during a search a 10-year-old boy had been spread-eagled on the stairs while soldiers trod on him, that religious objects had been thrown into the garden, and that implements kept by a blind woman for use in a workshop for the blind had been destroyed. The unit involved in the search was subsequently rung up by the householder in question, who said that, although a staunch pro-republican, none of these allegations had been made by her and she knew nothing of them.

IRA propaganda tactics are often subtle, and have sometimes included the imparting of false information designed to lead troops into needless harassing of the civilian population. The headquarters of one British infantry battalion was rung up by an anonymous caller and given the names and addresses of a number of men living in a particularly sensitive Catholic area of Belfast who, the caller alleged, were all active IRA supporters. A search party was sent to the area the next day on the basis of this information and of those named and taken in for questioning all were found to be innocent of any subversive activity. Meanwhile, considerable additional tension and anti-army feeling was created in the area by this apparently unjustified treatment of innocent citizens.

Army units with a particularly effective record of anti-terrorist operations have often been made a special target of persistent propaganda campaigns. A typical example was the various propaganda tactics employed against the Paratroop battalions. Early in 1972, stories were circulated in Ulster that senior officers of other regiments had complained to Army HQ about the case of brutality of paratroops during operations. These stories were later found to be completely untrue, but not before they had been

147

taken up by the Southern Irish and some of the British Press and reached a widespread audience.

IRA propaganda tactics have also shown a considerable flexibility, allowing for swift changes of approach if circumstances seem to demand it. At first, for instance, it was alleged that the death of thirteen people in Londonderry on 'Bloody Sunday' in February was due to British troops firing indiscriminately on a fleeing crowd. When it was seen from the fact that no women or children were amongst the casualties that the credibility of this story was low, an equally unfounded new version was introduced according to which there had been a conspiracy to shoot as many males of military age as possible.

Their propaganda efforts have been supplemented by the efforts of numbers of local defence committees under extremist control, by People's Democracy and by some sections of the Civil Rights movement. Considerable propaganda activity is carried on amongst school children who are urged to organize action committees, protest meetings and marches demanding the release of internees. One leaflet distributed in Belfast schools asking for action on behalf of internees was headed 'Action For Youth' and read, 'Do not delay longer, organize your school, it could be your father next.'

Branches of the Civil Rights Association have taken a leading part in organizing and encouraging opposition to both internment and arms searches. Very soon after the introduction of internment, the movement began to issue a daily 'emergency bulletin' which called on the Catholic population in Belfast to 'Resist—Resist!', stating that 'the NICRA calls upon people to show a united mass resistance to this temporary setback'. Leaflets issued by the movement in August 1972 urged residents in Catholic areas to take good care of their dustbin lids as they were needed to 'rattle a warning to your neighbours when . . . the British Army are launching search-out-and-destroy operations on your homes'.

URBAN GUERRILLA RULE

By early 1972 the Bogside and Creggan Estate areas of Londonderry represented enclaves unique in Western Europe and wholly under the control of revolutionary forces. The revolutionary garrison of members of both the Official and Provisional IRA were openly carrying arms, manning barricades and defence posts and steadily strengthening their defences, which by late spring included a Browning machine gun.

A system of street committees controlled the area and justice was meted out by IRA courts with a rough and ready system of punishment: warnings, 'punishment duty' such as street cleaning, tarring and feathering, shooting in the arms and legs, and death.

Some political education work was being carried on by the official IRA. Early in May it organized an 'education conference' for which its Chief of Staff Cathal Goulding came up from Dublin to speak on the history of Republicanism. The Official IRA also opened a co-operative shop, the stock of which was obtained from farmers and fishermen with whom they had made contact. The Provisional IRA, under its 21-year-old leader Martin McGuiness, who defined the aims of the Provisionals as being to fight for 'Democratic Socialism', were concentrating their political activity on plans for the holding of local elections. Michael Farrell of People's Democracy is said to have stated that Free Derry was like the Paris Commune, and that Marx would have given it his blessing.

The attraction of the 'no-go areas' as havens and operating bases were reported to be more and more apparent as the weeks went by to those many members of the IRA who had previously fled south across the border in the face of the successes obtained by the security forces in late 1971 and early 1972. It was thought that in addition to the comparative security they could count on in the Bogside and parts of Belfast, many of them were thinking of returning because of hopes that the British Government's promised 'political initiative' would result in a softer security policy being adopted than hitherto, thus providing a chance to rejoin the battle at less risk.

In this respect their hopes proved at least in part to be justi-fied; the 'low profile' policy imposed on the security forces after the introduction of direct rule had the result of producing a sharp fall in the number of casualties suffered by the IRA, and a sharp rise in the number of those suffered by the British Army and Ulster Police force. This was accompanied by an ever-escalating toll of material damage and civilian casualties. Its appalling culmination was on 'Bloody Friday', on 21 July. At the same time the consolidation of the no-go area in Londonderry, which began to take on the appearance of a revolutionary base, and the mushrooming of smaller such areas in Belfast, had the effect of drying up the army's flow of intelligence which had begun to produce such good results at the beginning of the year.

The subsequent elimination of the no-go areas took place without any of the mass bloodshed that had been feared, and the idea that the IRA intended to defend these areas in strength against vastly superior forces (and contrary to all the rules of guerrilla warfare) can now be doubted. The reintroduction of more vigorous measures following the liquidation of the no-go areas in Operation Motorman soon began to produce results in the succeeding months in the shape of a rapidly rising number of arms finds and arrests of leading members of the Provisional IRA, more than one of whom was found to have taken up arms again almost immediately upon his release from internment.

Despite this the scene remained a dark one, complicated by the appearance of the loyalist Ulster Defence Association and lightened only by the British Army's obvious ability to deal effectively with modern tactics of urban guerrilla warfare whenever politically inspired restrictions were lifted sufficiently to allow it to do so. By early autumn, the total number of deaths since the disturbances began had reached 600, and estimates of material damage the awe-inspiring figure of £66 million. When it is borne in mind that authoritative estimates have been given that the Provisional IRA can count on the active support of no more than 15 per cent of the Catholic population of Ulster, and even when allowances are made for the immense assistance the terrorists receive in the shape of the sanctuary and supply provided by the Irish Republic, it will be seen that the tragedy of Northern Ireland provides a remarkably vivid and ominous example of the immense damage that can be done to the fabric of a society, and the economy and life of a whole community, by modern revolutionaries operating within even a very small base, in terms of active public support.... A point that needs little emphasis when it is remembered that by the spring of 1973 fatal casualties in the province had reached a figure of nearly 800.

CHAPTER VII

International Aspects—The Helping Hands

Recent years have been remarkable for the steady growth in the number of sources to which leftward-looking revolutionary movements can look for some form of support and assistance.

Movements that operate in the Third World can now be reasonably certain of being able to obtain either arms, or the financial means to gain them, from the Soviet Bloc, Communist China, or, in the case of those operating in Latin America and some other areas, Cuba. Their revolutionary cadres may also be able to obtain training in guerrilla and subversive techniques in such countries, or instructors and 'advisers' may be sent to aid them in their homelands.

They can also almost certainly depend upon invaluable aid in making their causes known in the world through the immensely powerful propaganda machines of the entire 'socialist camp'. And in addition to these well-established centres of support active and would-be revolutionaries can now look in other directions for practical aid.

REVOLUTIONARY CENTRES

China

The first direct evidence of practical Communist Chinese support for revolutionary movements outside Asia came in 1961 when a party of Africans was arrested on return to the Cameroons. Questioning revealed that they had attended a ten-week course in guerrilla warfare at a military college near Peking. By the end of that year, the Peking *Chinese Daily* was claiming that Chinese-produced pamphlets on guerrilla warfare were circulating in many African countries. Since those days there has been a fairly continuous outward flow of arms and money from China to revolutionary movements in Asia, Africa and the Middle East and an inward flow of recruits from these areas going to China for training, although the latter was somewhat interrupted during the convulsions surrounding the Cultural Revolution.

China also provides a considerable amount of on-the-spot training by instructors and advisers in the base camps of guerrilla movements in their own or neighbouring countries. There are known to be a considerable number of Chinese instructors in camps in Tanzania, Zanzibar, Zambia and Congo-Brazzaville. The Chinese Embassy in Burundi was also at one time used as a base for the dispensation of clandestine funds and for instruction on revolutionary warfare.

Chinese links with guerrilla movements in the Middle East first became evident in 1965, when, under an arrangement with the Baathist Government, Chinese officers were attached to the Syrian Army for the purpose of training guerrillas for operations against Israel. Subsequently links were established through the Chinese mission in Damascus with the guerrilla coordinating group known as the Palestine Liberation Organization, based in Beirut. A PLO mission was set up in Peking, and in 1966 it was announced that a party of PLO guerrillas who had received training in China had 'returned to Arab territory' and that China was providing arms for the movement.

China has also extended her assistance to revolutionary groups in the area of the Persian Gulf, which since the British withdrawal have established bases in Aden. Chief among these has been the Popular Front for the Liberation of the Occupied Arab Gulf (PFLOAG), whose guerrillas have been active in Oman. Considerable publicity has been given to the activities of these guerrillas by the New China News Agency and Peking Radio, and in 1970 a number of its members visited China on a tour which received elaborate news coverage.

There is evidence that some Western revolutionaries have

received at least paramilitary training in China's forward European base, Albania. The Chinese Embassy in Switzerland was at one time an important centre for Chinese contact with Western European Maoist movements. After the recognition of the Peking government by France, however, its importance became transcended by the new embassy in Paris, but Maoist activities have also been coordinated from Brussels. Enormous quantities of propaganda literature, much of it of a highly subversive and inflammatory nature, are despatched each year for sale through Maoist bookshops all over the non-Communist world. These are often strongly linked to Chinese embassies, where these exist.

In Asia, as well as providing continuous and invaluable support for the Viet Cong and its allied Communist revolutionary movements in Cambodia and Laos, China has afforded assistance to the Naga and Mizo tribesmen engaged in revolutionary conflict on the borders of India, to the 'White Flag Communists' in Burma and Maoist guerrillas in the Philippines.

Cuba

The Government of Cuba has never made any secret of its desire to promote revolution throughout the Latin American area, or of its sympathy for revolutionary movements in other parts of the world. Only shortly after the revolutionary government had itself been established on the island, recruits from a number of countries of the Southern half of the American continent were arriving to receive instruction in the political and military techniques of revolt.

Such training has been mainly conducted in the Guerrilla Academy at Minas Del Frio, where students not only from all over South America but also from many other parts of the world have received instruction. It has been estimated that between 100 and 200 Africans a year alone have passed through the Academy. By 1970 a total of at least 5,000 foreigners had received training in Cuba. It would seem that some of these trainees have included a few young revolutionaries from the United States and Western Europe. One member of the Maoist Progressive Labour Party testified that he had been instructed in the use of explosives by an expert, a major in the North Vietnamese army, whilst there, and had then returned to the United States where he kept in close touch with Cuban diplomats at the United Nations. According to one report a former member of the British Army now involved in the direction of the Irish Republican Army's bombing campaign in Northern Ireland learnt his terrorist techniques in Cuba.

Cuba also provides on-the-spot training, sending instructors attached to foreign-based guerrilla movements, notably in Congo-Brazzaville, where their presence has been noticed for some years.

Since 1966 much of the Cuban Government's efforts in the field of subversion and promoting revolutionary movements has been carried on through the Tri-Continental Solidarity Organization; a nominally independent, but in fact completely Government-controlled organization with headquarters in Havana. Included within its organization are a Committee to Aid the Liberation Movements, whose terms of reference are:

'To unite, coordinate and develop the struggle of the peoples of Africa, Asia and Latin America against imperialism, colonialism and neo-colonialism, headed by U.S. imperialism, and to organize the flow of aid to National Liberation Movements and newly independent countries.'[1]

The Soviet Bloc

The Soviet Union officially claims that it does not believe in exporting revolution, but nevertheless does have contact with guerrilla movements in Asia, Africa, and Latin America, and provides practical aid for not a few.

The main centre for the training of guerrillas in the Soviet Union is in Simferopol in the Crimea. A camp here can hold over 400 trainees at one time, and the training provided includes mine-laying, ambush techniques, fire coordination and the general tactics of revolutionary warfare, as well as instruction in topography, driving, and even wireless and television techniques. Most of the trainees are Africans and members of the various guerrilla movements engaged in operations against Portuguese rule in Angola, Moçambique and Guinea. A particularly large share of

[1] Lionel Sotto, 'First Conference of the People of Three Continents', *World Marxist Review*, April 1966, pp. 1–6

the Soviet Union's training and supply facilities are made available to the Movimento Popular de Libertaçao de Angola, (MPLA) and the Frente de Libertaçao de Moçambique (FRELIMO). Large numbers of Africans from the Zambian Zimbabwe African People's Union (ZAPU), which aims to overturn the present government of Rhodesia by revolutionary means, and of the African National Congress (ANC) which aims to bring about a revolution in South Africa, have also undergone training in Simferopol and at an intelligence school in Moscow. Other Africans have received training in Bulgaria and in East Germany.

The Africans involved are usually recruited in their home countries by a personal approach from an agent of the guerrilla movement concerned. Quite often the real purpose of their recruitment is not revealed, but they are offered an educational course abroad for which all travelling expenses will be paid. If they accept this or similar offers they are then taken to camps for recruits and there kept under special observation for a period. Those that seem the most promising material are then sent on for training in the Soviet Union or some other Communist country.

Another source of recruitment for guerrilla training is from among the Third World students attending ordinary university civil courses of instruction in Moscow. The Soviet Union has recently been involved in the training of guerrilla recruits from Mexico, although elaborate plans were taken to try to disguise the Soviet Union's participation in the operation and military training for the recruits actually was provided in North Korea as a part of this camouflage.

The Soviet Bloc as a whole provided instructors in guerrilla and intelligence methods to serve in guerrilla base camps in Africa, particularly in Ghana during the days of Dr Nkrumah's régime, and later in Zanzibar; many of the instructors have come from East Germany. In the Middle East the Soviet Union sponsored the formation of a guerrilla group known as *Ansar* (partisans), but the main role of this seems to have been not action on its own account but infiltration of the various other anti-Israel movements in the area. East German experts now advise the police force of the revolutionary Government of Aden.

Probably the most important aid received from the Soviet Bloc

155

is the immense quantities of arms supplied to guerrilla groups all over the world. A large percentage are of Czechoslovakian manufacture, and are despatched through the Czech State trading company Omnipol. In the few cases in which direct payment is demanded the price asked is almost always considerably below the normal market rate. Since the mid-1950s Soviet Bloc arms have been found in the hands of guerrillas in almost all Third World countries in which serious revolt has taken place. Particularly large quantities of arms were despatched for the use of the Viet Minh in Indo-China from about 1952 onwards, and the Soviet Bloc subsequently became responsible for providing two-thirds of the war needs of North Vietnam and the Viet Cong. The FLN in Algeria received vast quantities of arms from the Soviet Bloc. Soviet leaders openly boasted of their willingness to supply arms for the use of Egyptian-backed terrorists against British troops in Aden. The exact circumstances in which a large consignment of Czechoslovakian small arms was consigned to agents of the Provisional IRA in the autumn of 1971 have not yet been fully clarified; no more than at the time of writing has the arrival of RPG-7 anti-tank rockets of Soviet make in the hands of the same force late in 1972.

As well as what might be described as the primary centres of moral and logistic support for today's revolutionaries, a number of secondary centres of increasing impact have made their appearance during recent years.

Algeria

A large guerrilla training camp is maintained at the old FLN revolutionary training ground of Telmecen. Large numbers from Angolan guerrilla movements as well as many recruits from other African countries have received training there. At one time the Chinese Government offered to pay the expenses of members of Rhodesian nationalist movements to go to this base for training. The city of Algiers houses the headquarters of a number of small revolutionary movements from Africa and elsewhere. In one of the more select suburbs the headquarters of the 'International Section' of the U.S. Black Panther party are located in a villa whose previous occupants were the mission of the National Liberation Front of South Vietnam. The Black Panthers' International Section is presided over by Eldridge Cleaver who, from this base on the edge of the Mediterranean, is planning to build a world-wide Black Power movement. Algiers has also become a convenient refuge and temporary base for prominent revolutionaries on the run from South and North America, particularly a number of leading Weathermen including Bernadette Dorhn, as well as being the headquarters of the illegal Portuguese Communist Party.

The Middle East Guerrilla Camps

The training camps maintained by the various Arab guerrilla groups formed for the purpose of carrying on irregular warfare and terrorism against Israel have, it would seem, been attended by considerable numbers of students from outside the Arab world intent on learning the arts of People's War, and the influence of these individual movements on the international revolutionary movement as a whole is consequently far-reaching.

With the exception of the oldest, Al Fatah, whose leadership has up to date been of a comparatively right-wing nature, the movements which maintain these camps are Marxist and revolutionary in outlook, believing that the destruction of the state of Israel in its present form should be accompanied by revolts against most established régimes throughout the Arab world, as part of the universal revolt against capitalist and imperialist 'domination'. One of the most extreme is Al Saika (The Thunderbolt), a pro-Baathist movement based in Syria. It is dedicated to helping establish a democratic Arab state in Palestine, and subsequently a greater Arab socialist state covering all the Eastern Arab countries. The syllabus in this movement's officer training schools consists largely of lectures based on the experience of revolutionary forces in China, Vietnam, Cuba, and Yugoslavia. Political Commissars are responsible for overseeing political education within its ranks in all its units and bases. This group has strong links with Syrian army intelligence.

An overtly Marxist group is the Popular Democratic Front for the Liberation of Palestine, which was formed in 1969. Its policies are based on the theory that it will not be possible to solve the Palestine problem without at the same time trying to deal with serious problems facing Arab countries themselves, and bringing about a social revolution throughout the Arab world. Based in Jordan, the PDFLP maintains a number of training camps, and information is divided into two phases; the first is concerned with the 'Palestine problem'; in the second the emphasis is on general problems connected with the mounting of revolution. As with Al Saika lectures are given on the lessons learned by revolutionaries in Vietnam and other countries, and discussions are also held on the reasons why certain revolutions, for instance that in Algeria, have not culminated in 'a radical social transformation'. In addition to obligatory periods of military training there is also instruction in such subjects as basic economics. The group's training and political education programme also includes special courses on the following subjects: revolutionary organization, including both legal and clandestine activities; an analysis of the class structure in the Arab countries and the prospect for revolution within them; and the prospects for the development of revolutionary situations on a world-wide scale.

The group which probably has the most sophisticated system of political and military training is the Popular Front for the Liberation of Palestine (PFLP), the leader of which, George Habash, has described himself as an 'Asiatic Marxist-Leninist'. Based in Beirut, it has a special school for cadres, at which courses last for about five months, longer than those run by any other group. The purpose of the course is to produce cadres capable of forming and managing revolutionary cells and bases, and of planning guerrilla campaigns in both rural or urban settings. Alternate weeks of the course are given over to military and political training. In the political curriculum comes Marxist-Leninist theory, Marxist philosophy, study of the Communist Manifesto, the writings of Marx, Engels, and Lenin, the revolution in China, Korea, Vietnam and Cuba, the workers' movement in Europe, the strategy of wars of liberation, the relations between Communist countries and the Third World, and national liberation movements and neo-colonialism. As well as practical instruction the military training schedule includes a close study of the writings of Clausewitz, and the tactical and strategic theories of Mao Tse-tung and General Giap.

Factual information about the number of non-Arab revolutionaries training in guerrilla camps in Syria and Jordan is scanty, but there is no doubt that some have done so, and that some of these have been Africans and Latin Americans; although it would seem that most of these have been attending courses as individuals rather than as members of any organization. Since about 1969 parties from various West European revolutionary movements have paid short visits to some of the camps, and to at least one run by Al Fatah, which despite its 'conservative' leadership does contain some Marxist elements, but these would seem to have been more in the nature of goodwill missions than serious attempts to obtain training. Two members of the French-Canadian FLQ were observed in a camp run by the Popular Democratic Front for the Liberation of Palestine in Jordan in August 1970 and stated that 'we are learning more how to kill than how to mobilize popular movements', and that the particular object of their training was to become experts at 'selective assassination'. The same year members of the FLQ attempted to organize a Quebec-Palestine solidarity week in conjunction with Al Fatah, but this plan came to nothing. A small number of members of the American Black Panther Movement were also in Jordan camps in 1970. It is known that members of the West German Baader-Meinhof Group and the Turkish People's Liberation Army have received training in Middle East camps. There have also been reliable reports of contacts between representatives of Al Fatah and the Provisional IRA.

Al Fatah is probably the wealthiest of the Arab guerrilla groups: it is estimated that it has funds amounting to £2 million at its disposal. It believes that 'revolutionary violence exerted by the masses' is the only way of liberating 'the homeland'. Presided over by a Central Committee, its somewhat complex organization embraces a Political Bureau, a Military Bureau, and an Information Centre. It works largely through a system of cells in refugee camps, factories, and universities. An offshoot of Al Fatah of growing importance is the notorious Black September group whose activities are summarized in chapter eight.

Early in December 1972, the *New York Times* stated in a report from Beirut that a special organization was to be set up to channel aid to the Arab groups from the Soviet Bloc. Active Soviet interest in these groups was revealed in 1970 when Yassir Arafat, the leader of both Al Fatah and the Palestine Liberation

Organization (the latter being the political arm and coordinating body of the Palestinian groups), paid his first official visit to Moscow. It transpired that he had in fact paid several 'private' visits to the Soviet capital over the previous two years. According to the *New York Times*, a conference attended by delegates from twenty countries and held in Beirut decided to set up the new body under the title of the Arab Front for Participation in the Palestinian Resistance. Amongst those attending were representatives from the Communist parties of the Soviet Union, Hungary, Poland, East Germany, Bulgaria, Rumania and Yugoslavia. Representatives of the ruling parties of Algeria, Iraq, and Syria, and the Lebanese Communist party were also said to be present. The conference also passed a resolution calling for a joint Palestinian-Jordanian effort to bring about the overthrow of King Hussein.

North Korea

North Korea has for some years been attempting to launch a guerrilla war in the southern half of the country and has a number of guerrilla warfare camps within its boundaries, some of which have been attended by foreign students from Africa and other parts of the Third World.

An elaborate Soviet-sponsored plan to use North Korea as a training ground for recruits for a guerrilla force recruited in Mexico was revealed by the defection of a woman member of the staff of the Mexican Soviet Embassy. Recruits for the nucleus of the guerrilla force, with which it was hoped to launch a major guerrilla campaign on the doorstep of the United States, were enlisted by some of the many Soviet intelligence agents working under diplomatic cover at the Mexico Embassy. A selected number, most of whom came largely from the ranks of discontented students, were then flown to Moscow ostensibly for normal educational courses. From Moscow they were flown on to North Korea, and there underwent intensive training in guerrilla techniques before being imported back into Mexico with the aim of setting up a network of revolutionary cells and preparing for the establishment of a guerrilla base.

North Korea has also established links with a number of guerrilla groups in Africa; including those operating in Moçambique, Portuguese Guinea, Rhodesia and South West Africa. A number of delegations from these movements have visited North Korea over recent years, and it would seem that training facilities have been provided for African revolutionaries for some considerable time. For instance, one Kenyan student arrested in 1969 in possession of plans for a projected full-scale anti-government revolt, admitted having received training in guerrilla techniques in North Korea five years before. In 1971 relations between North Korea and the Central African Republic were severed, after the disclosure of anti-Government activities by North Korean diplomats based in the Central African Republic's capital city of Bangui. The North Korean Deputy Chief of Staff visited Al Fatah in mid-1970. He was reported to have expressed his country's full support for the Palestinian groups; the same year Dr George Habash visited North Korea.

North Vietnam

The efforts of North Vietnam in propagating revolution have been concentrated, in addition to its mammoth efforts in the war in the south, to training and equipping Communist guerrilla forces in Laos, Cambodia and Thailand. Its influence as a revolutionary centre has, however, also been felt much farther afield, and not purely through propaganda or the writings of the commander of its army, General Giap, which have become required reading for revolutionaries all over the world. As early as 1962, Western intelligence officers discovered documents indicating that North Vietnamese agents had given advice on guerrilla warfare tactics to terrorist movements in Portuguese Guinea and the Kwiliu province of the Congo. Reports have spoken of American students receiving instruction from North Vietnamese Army explosive experts in Cuba; and the leader of one Palestinian guerrilla group has stated that one of his aides received training in North Vietnam.

REVOLUTION AND INTERNATIONAL PROPAGANDA— THE ORTHODOX COMMUNIST NETWORK

Any revolutionary movement of the left that does not deviate too far along the path of Maoism or Trotskyism, and which can claim to be fighting against colonialism, neo-colonialism, or imperialism, can be virtually certain of receiving sympathetic support from the orthodox Moscow-aligned Communist propaganda machine, the Soviet Union's foreign broadcasting and other propaganda services, the various international Communist front organizations with headquarters based in Eastern Europe, local Communist parties, and their various front organizations. The amount of support given to any particular movement is dependent mainly upon the closeness of its policy to the orthodox Communist line, and upon its long-term chance of success and its probable value in assisting the general cause of the destruction of the capitalist system. The fact that the Soviet Government may ostensibly enjoy friendly relations with a government against which a revolt is in progress is not usually any bar to propaganda support by Moscow for those engaged in the revolt.

The Soviet Union has for some years led the world in the field of foreign language broadcasting in the number of hours broadcast per week. The main channel has been Radio Moscow whose programmes in the past have often carried items consisting of open encouragement and support for revolt in particular countries. More recently, however, it would seem that this role has been largely taken over by a new and powerful station, Radio Peace and Progress; this is officially said to be run by an independent organization, but in fact is no less under Government supervision than Radio Moscow, the sole reason for its establishment apparently being to allow the Soviet Foreign Ministry to disavow the highly inflammatory and subversive tone of its broadcasts with some show of plausibility. Radio Peace and Freedom broadcasts have aroused strong protests from the governments of countries as far apart as Latin America and India.

The Soviet Union has also allowed its territory or that of its subordinate allies in Eastern Europe to be used as bases for pirate, or 'black', radio stations. These are usually manned by exiled members of some Communist party which is illegal in its homeland, and which is hoping to launch an eventual revolt within it in order to obtain power. Such stations normally pretend to be broadcasting from within the country to which they are beamed. Examples of such stations are those broadcasting to Spain, Greece, Turkey and Iran.

Vast quantities of literature, from elaborately produced books to cheap pamphlets, have been produced in many different languages by the state-controlled publishing houses of the Soviet Union and other Eastern European states, stressing the need for 'wars of liberation' to remove the last remnants of imperialism and neo-colonialism from the world, and extolling the heroism of those who take part in such campaigns. Massive quantities of such literature are exported to the non-Communist world and sold at cut-price rates through Communist-controlled or left-wing bookshops, and through information centres connected with embassies.

An essential role is played by the Soviet Union's two foreign news agencies, Tass and Novosti. The editorial offices of many Communist Party journals in non-Communist countries have a direct tele-type link with the Moscow headquarters of Tass and the agency supplies a considerable amount of the foreign news reported by them. Prominence is given in Tass reportage to the activities of favoured revolutionary movements and armies of liberation, and consequently reports of their doings based on this source are frequently given important place in the Communist press all over the world. The Novosti news agency's primary task is the circulation of feature articles, photographs and pamphlets and booklets. Again a considerable proportion of the subject matter is concerned with 'wars of liberation', or anti-imperialist campaigns of any description.

Communist parties play an invaluable part in rallying public opinion in their respective countries in support of movements involved in 'armed struggle' against 'reactionary governments' in other lands. The prime example is the efforts of Communist parties round the world to popularize the cause of the National Liberation Front in South Vietnam, but there have been other instances, notably the French Communist Party's work during the war in Indo-China and in the later stages of the Algerian campaign. One of the main tactics used is the organizing of mass demonstrations, and sometimes efforts have been also made to promote industrial action as a gesture of symbolic support for some particular revolutionary cause, but these have seldom been attended with much success. But considerable success has undoubtedly been obtained by more subtle tactics in the influence brought to bear by 'fellow-travellers' or concealed party members

163

working in the news media and other opinion-moulding fields.

In like manner the various front organizations which invariably operate in conjunction with Communist parties play a most valuable part, producing a considerable volume of protest deputations, special literature and statements, all from organizations which as far as the general public are concerned appear to be independent and to reflect unbiased opinion, but all of which in fact speak with the Communist voice. The international fronts fulfil a similar role on a world-wide scale. Those most active in arousing support for revolutionary movement are the World Peace Council (WPC), the World Federation of Democratic Youth (WFDY), and the International Union of Students (IUS), all having their headquarters behind the iron curtain with ample staffs and funds at their disposal. These three organizations have between them played a key part in organizing the long series of international conferences which have taken place in order to arouse public opinion and plan protest action against American participation in the war in Vietnam.

As well as these, other international fronts can be made to play a useful part in supporting the revolutionary cause. The International Association of Democratic Lawyers can, for instance, be relied upon to produce timely resolutions condemning some alleged excess of government forces engaged in fighting revolt, or in condemning them or their allies for some alleged breach of international law. The World Federation of Scientific Workers can in similar fashion be prevailed upon to produce damaging allegations concerning the use by security forces of illegal weapons such as gas or germ warfare.

Although the nature and complexion of the international fronts has long been known, statements and declarations by them continue to be quite often printed in the non-communist press without any words of explanation as to their background, giving the impression that these pronouncements are indeed the unsolicited opinions of uncommitted impartial experts.

THE MAOIST AND TROTSKYIST NETWORK

The Maoist international propaganda network functions in very much the same fashion as that of Soviet Communism, except that Peking and not Moscow lies at the centre of the net, and their encouragement and support for violence are more overt and flamboyant. Technically the Communist Chinese propaganda output nearly matches, and in some respects may surpass, that of the Soviet Union.

The tendency of Maoist parties to splinter into numerous small groups, each somehow capable of producing considerable quantities of propaganda material, means that the Maoist point of view is often well represented in terms of locally produced literature, despite the fact that the total number of Maoists in any given country may only be very small. On the whole the Maoist attitude towards revolts that are under way under other than Maoist leadership is one of general support, accompanied by a constant stressing of the practical and ideological advantages of it becoming a 'real', or Maoist, revolution as soon as possible.

Until recently there was little evidence of practical cooperation between Trotskyist organizations in different countries, but the revitalization of the IV International is beginning to change this, and various Trotskyist-aligned groups, such as the International Socialists in Britain, have foreign contacts of their own. Trotskyists are very well aware of the importance of propaganda, and have played a particularly active part in the anti-Vietnam War movement, largely dominating the more extreme sections of it in Britain, France and America. The Trotskyist press devotes considerable space to the activities of revolutionary movements in action in different areas of the world, and meetings are frequently called by Trotskyist organizations to express support and solidarity.

In addition the cause of 'world revolution' is also aided, both wittingly and unwittingly, in its propaganda by a whole further assortment of organizations and groups. These include the ultra-liberals, well-intentioned persons who dislike the type of régime in power in particular countries so much that they are prepared to devote great energy and often considerable funds to helping secure their destruction, without giving much thought to the type of régime that is likely to take the place of the existing one. The underground press that now exists in most Western countries also gives valuable aid in bringing revolutionary activities and ideology to the notice of a section of the population who would probably not bother to read purely political publications. Finally, there are a number of 'special news' and counter-media groups and most importantly the foreign offices maintained by the political wings of guerrilla forces in the field, such as those of the NLF of South Vietnam.

PROPAGANDA IN THE SERVICE OF TERROR

In 1970 Cathal Goulding was asked in the course of an interview if his organization favoured a worldwide campaign for the withdrawal of British troops from Northern Ireland, and replied:

'We do favour such a campaign and we are trying to develop one particularly through our allies in America, the people who are organizing the different Irish emigrant groups in America. We are trying to get these people to work as much as possible to publicize why the British troops are in Ireland, what they are doing and what they are protecting. We have Irish organizations in Australia, New Zealand, America, and England. We have also established contact with other countries where there are socialist groups and we are trying to work with these people to arouse worldwide feeling against the occupation of Ireland by England.'[2]

At the same time Tomas MacGiolla, President of the section of Sinn Fein attached to the Officials, said that he and his colleagues had become very much aware of the growth of the anti-war movement in America and the 'influence which it has in restraining the designs of the Washington government.'[3] He continued:

'We are convinced that this movement can be most helpful to a small nation like Ireland if it were engaged in a struggle for its national liberation such as the Vietnamese people are engaged in at the moment...'

In point of fact, the IRA really needed no lessons in the importance of a successful international propaganda campaign to revolutionaries; the record of the Irish Republican movement has always shown a great awareness of the importance of this weapon. Efforts to arouse support from amongst Irish immigrants

[2] Gerry Foley, *Ireland in Rebellion*, Pathfinder Press (New York, 1971), p. 23
[3] Ibid., p. 30

in America began well before the First World War. In 1914 an Irish-American organization which was to have a continuing importance, the Clann Na Gael, set up a committee for the purpose of organizing and equipping an expeditionary force to go to Ireland. During the war years the same organization cooperated with the German Ambassador in the USA in schemes to import German arms into Ireland to aid Sir Roger Casement's rising.

After the failure of the 1916 rising, the Clann established an 'Irish Victory Fund', which in the next four years collected nearly $900,000 in aid of the cause. Further propaganda efforts in America directed by Mr De Valera himself resulted in the raising of over $5 million through the sale of bonds redeemable on Irish independence.

A special organization for the dissemination of atrocity stories regarding British rule and the British Army, the American Commission on Conditions in Ireland, was established. Nationalist funds were further augmented by the operations of an organization of a type which has since become familiar, the American Committee for Relief in Ireland. There is reason to believe that the bulk of the funds collected by the Committee went, not for relief, but towards the nationalist war effort.

The establishment of the Irish Free State by no means satisfied the ambitions of Clann Na Gael, which continued to pursue a campaign devoted to the eradication of British control and influence throughout Ireland. Although its activities became somewhat diverted to the illegal sale of Irish sweepstake tickets in the latter interwar years, it was reformed in 1945 as a semi-secret and highly political organization. New members had to go through an elaborate initiation ceremony and to swear the following oath:

> 'I ... do solemnly swear that I will labour while life is left in me to put an end to English rule in Ireland and to sustain the Republic on Irish soil and to elevate the position of the Irish race everywhere ... That I will never reveal its [the Clann's] secrets to anyone not entitled to know them, even if my connection with the organization should cease from any cause whatever.'[4]

[4] Tim Pat Coogan, *I.R.A.*, Fontana (London, 1971). p. 147

When the IRA border campaign commenced in 1958, the Clann Na Gael again became a major base of financial and material support and so continues today. Whilst the Clann retains influence amongst the older Irish-American generation it is probable that support from younger people is tapped by more radical organizations like the Association for Justice in Northern Ireland which, led by James Connolly's grandson, Brian Heron, openly supports the Provisional IRA and their tactics, and which spreads its activities all over the United States through sixty different chapters. It has claimed to have raised more than £100,000 for the IRA in two years.

Another organization performing a similar function is the National Association for Irish Freedom, which works in support of the Official IRA and the Northern Ireland Civil Rights Association. There are also many smaller organizations devoted to giving support to the cause.

The fires of anti-British feeling over the Irish question and the fervour of pro-IRA supporters in both the United States and Europe are kept regularly stoked by the visits of leading members of both wings of the IRA or their political supporters on lecture tours. Typical of such tours was one undertaken by Malachy McGurran, Vice-President of the Official wing of Sinn Fein in the spring of 1972. The tour started off with a visit to Paris, where McGurran spoke at several meetings organized by left-wing groups, receiving a particularly warm welcome at one arranged by the Strollard Kommunour Breizh, a revolutionary organization based in Brittany, but which also has many members in the Paris area. McGurran then proceeded to Scandinavia to meet speaking engagements in Denmark, Sweden and Norway. The main theme of his speeches was that events in Ireland should not be viewed as a religious war but as a revolutionary one, and the Official IRA wanted and were preparing for revolution embracing the whole of Ireland.

Reporting this tour the *United Irishman*, organ of the Official IRA, stated that whereas an organization known as the Nordirlandsgruppen had for some time been carrying on a propaganda campaign in Sweden in support of the Northern Irish Civil Rights movement, it was now intended to set up new solidarity organizations which would 'primarily be support groups for the Republican Movement expressing a more socialist character'. It apparently was envisaged that these organizations should take the form of Republican Clubs in various Swedish towns. An organization dedicated to support for the IRA has since been set up in West Germany.

A pro-IRA point of view has been so firmly established in some sections of the Swedish press that it is now difficult for journalists to get articles published that give a less than favourable impression of its activities. A reporter who had lived in Ulster and wanted to criticize Provisional IRA tactics had his articles rejected on the grounds that the paper to which he subjected them felt that such opinions would be at variance with those of the leader pages, and that anyway the paper was in favour of 'progressive violence'. Another paper rejected them on the grounds that the television services had been proclaiming the IRA to be heroes for months and it was not possible to go against the general impression that had been formed. One British observer in Sweden has remarked that the IRA seemed to be increasingly taking the place of the Viet Cong as an object of hero-worship; and that it was noticeable that the same groups that had in the past supported the Viet Cong now supported the IRA as well.

The Provisional IRA investment in contacts with the Trotskyist International soon showed dividends in the way of propaganda support in Europe. Early in 1972 a series of meetings was arranged in Belgian universities with the help of the IV International on the subject of 'Ireland and the Armed Struggle in Europe'. In spite of an attempted ban on the meetings by the Belgian police, gatherings did in fact take place and were addressed by, amongst others, Gerry Lawless, the leading member of the IV International's British affiliate, the International Marxist Group, and former member of an IRA splinter group. According to a British Trotskyist journal speakers stressed the need to:

> 'build campaigns in solidarity with the struggle of the Irish people and its armed vanguard, the IRA. As the result of these meetings the prospects of a significant Irish Solidarity Campaign in Belgium are now extremely good.'[5]

Following the shooting of thirteen people in Londonderry, a

[5] *Red Mole*, March 1971

number of well-publicized demonstrations were organized by organizations affiliated to the IV International in European cities, including Paris, West Berlin and Stockholm. Two months later Tariq Ali of the International Marxist Group paid an illegal visit to Paris to take part in a press conference together with leading Belgian and French Trotskyists. During the course of the conference he said that Ireland's entry into the Common Market would mean that the war between the IRA and Britain would continue on a European scale. But contacts between the IRA and representatives of the IV International have not been confined to the former's Provisional wing. The International Marxist Group has, for instance, played an important part in helping with arrangements for one tour of North America by a speaker of the Official IRA.

The scope of the pro-IRA campaign in Europe has become ever more extensive and has included the publication of much propaganda material alleging British misdeeds and extolling the virtues of the Freedom Fighters of the Bogside and Belfast. One such publication was printed in English by the Communist Party in West Berlin, carrying on its cover a picture of British troops in action at a street barricade, together with the slogan 'Get these gunmen out of Ireland'. The publication carried potted histories of the IRA and other anti-unionist movements in Northern Ireland.

In Britain similar propaganda is disseminated by the Connolly Association which has strong links with the Official IRA, and the Association has been described by one of its ex-founder-members as having been 'nothing more or less' than a Communist front since the mid-1930s. Clan Na H'Eireann, which was formed in 1962, is another organization advocating support for the Official IRA in Britain. Its President, Seamus Collins, has described himself as a 'groping Marxist'. Although it is most active in areas with a high population of Irish immigrants, it aims to try to obtain the maximum possible support from English people. It works very closely with various ultra-left groups and in some trade unions and universities.

Clan Na H'Eireann claims to have branches in most large cities in Britain and to have several hundred members. It has also claimed to have sent 'thousands of pounds' to Dublin for the use of the Republican cause.

Two other organizations playing a major part in agitation against British policy in Ireland are the Irish Solidarity Campaign, and the Anti-Internment League which is led by Gerry Lawless. The Irish Solidarity Campaign works through a number of branches throughout Britain. The influence of both the International Marxist Group and the International Socialists is strong in its ranks, and it has been described as:

'A unique organization: neither an Irish organization in Britain, nor an organization of British people in solidarity with the Irish struggle, it is an attempt to combine both of these and make use of the links between the two to grease the slope of British imperialism's decline.'

It has some branches in universities and publishes its own paper, the *Irish Citizen*. It believes in a policy of 'principled support' for the IRA.

The Anti-Internment League was formed just after the introduction of internment in Northern Ireland in the summer of 1971. It is led by a member of People's Democracy, John Grey, and is an 'umbrella' organization to which a large number of other bodies are affiliated. These include Clan Na H'Eireann, the provisional wing of Sinn Fein, People's Democracy, Irish Solidarity Campaign, Northern Ireland Civil Rights Association, International Socialists, International Marxist Group, the Independent Labour Party, the Communist Party of Great Britain Marxist-Leninist, and the National Union of Students, which gives qualified support to the IRA. The Anti-Internment League has been responsible for organizing a number of large-scale demonstrations in London and elsewhere.

PROPAGANDA IN SPATE

The concerted campaign throughout the world against American intervention in the Vietnamese war and on behalf of Victory for the Viet Cong provides without doubt the prime example of the use of international propaganda in pursuit of a revolutionary cause. The awareness of the Viet Cong and their political masters of the power of propaganda, the eagerness of leaders of revolutionary groups and Communist parties in the free world to exploit the situation by picturing the war as a vivid example of 'imperialist oppression', the importance given by the

Communist powers to victory crowning the efforts of those they support, and the horror of genuine pacifist opinion at the protracted nature of the grim struggle; all have combined to produce an enormous weight of propaganda which has already greatly affected the course of the war and could be decisive as to its outcome.

Their campaign has been based on three distinct channels: first through propaganda directed by the foreign propaganda department of the Viet Cong's political arm, the National Liberation Front of South Vietnam, and by the Government of North Vietnam in Hanoi; secondly, by the foreign propaganda services of Communist China and the Soviet Bloc and the front organizations under these sources' control; and thirdly, by a host of pressure groups working within the countries of the non-Communist world.

The National Liberation Front maintains some fifteen missions of various types in non-Communist countries, including embassies in Algeria, Egypt, the Sudan, Syria, Tanzania and South Yemen and Iraq. In Western Europe it is represented through a chain of information bureaux in Paris, Sweden, Denmark and Norway. The NLF Embassy in East Berlin also plays an important role as a coordinating centre for propaganda activities in Europe.

Backing the efforts of these foreign missions are important home-based weapons such as the broadcasting services of Radio Hanoi and the output of Hanoi's Foreign Language publishing house, which publishes very large quantities of literature in the languages of non-Communist countries for dissemination through overseas missions, left-wing bookshops and so on. Typical of its products is a book entitled *Letters From South Vietnam*, supposedly a collection of letters written by members of the Viet Cong and its supporting organizations to their families; part of the foreword reads:

'Letters from South Vietnam (Vol. 11) is in your hands! Here are letters written within range of the enemy guns, in prison, in the forest, in the field, on the seashore, at a street corner, in a sampan, on horseback, in a dug-out ... They might be written at a table of a mass organization office, or in the headquarters of the guerrilla forces. In writing them their authors do not think of literature and art. They only want to depict a reality which they have witnessed, describe the feats which they have accomplished and all from the bottom of their hearts.

'We hope that this sincerity will inspire in our readers a profound sympathy for the just struggle of our South Vietnam compatriots.'

The activities of NLF missions abroad can be glimpsed from that of its information mission in Sweden, a country in which anti-American and pro-Viet Cong feeling has been maintained at a high pitch. The office in Stockholm has a full-time staff of five Vietnamese with paid and volunteer local helpers in addition. Their main propaganda weapon is the film: twenty-eight different films, some of them in colour, are exhibited at shows and meetings all over Sweden. Members of the office staff also address many meetings, take part in the organization of demonstrations and rallies, and work closely with the various extremely active pro-Viet Cong groups in the country, and with the special organization run by deserters from the American armed forces, of whom over 300 have taken refuge in Sweden.

The power of the overseas propaganda machine of Communist China and the Soviet Bloc has been summarized earlier in this chapter, and these have been fully harnessed to the service of the Vietnam campaign. Probably the most effective part has been played by the international fronts, especially those dedicated to appealing to pacifist sentiment and to agitation amongst youth.

This activity saw a great intensification from 1967 onwards. In March 1968 the World Federation of Democratic Youth and the International Union of Students launched a World Movement of Youth for the Victory of the Vietnamese People. In the same year a Conference of the Western Hemisphere to End the US War in Vietnam was sponsored by the Canadian Peace Partisans movement, an affiliate of the World Peace Council. It took place in Montreal and was attended by over 2,000 representatives of various professional bodies from both North and South America, as well as delegations from both the NLF and North Vietnam.

In November 1968 the International Union of Students initiated a 'Week of International Solidarity of the Students with the Heroic Struggle of the Vietnamese People against American Aggression', and demonstrations, exhibitions and meetings on

Vietnam were held in many countries during this and the following weeks. The International Union of Students secretariat issued a special appeal at this time to world student organizations to redouble their efforts in support of the Vietnamese people.

At the end of 1968, a delegation of the International Union of Students visited North Vietnam, where its Secretary General emphasized its determination to step up support.

In the autumn of 1969, the World Federation of Democratic Youth and the International Union of Students combined to hold a 'World Meeting of Youth and Students for Final Victory of the Vietnamese People, for Independence and Peace'. It was claimed that 215 youth delegations from seventy-eight different countries attended this conference, at which recommendations for the staging of a 'world-wide youth and students' campaign in support of the Vietnamese people' were made. A regional conference on Vietnam for Asian youth and students was then held by the two organizations in New Delhi in December.

It would seem that much of the preliminary planning for anti-war demonstrations that took place in North America during 1970 was done at a semi-secret meeting held in January of that year in a hotel in the Laurentian mountains near St Jerome, Quebec. It was attended by representatives of the Communist Party of Canada, the Communist Party of the United States, the German Peace Society, the Black Panthers, the World Peace Council, and a number of other groups. A delegation from the NLF was once again present. This was followed by a World Conference on Vietnam held in Stockholm in November 1970, sponsored by the World Peace Council. Delegations from sixty different countries were present and a commission presented a programme of action designed to 'bring disaster to the United States'. The World Council of Peace Assembly held in Budapest in May 1971 was attended by twenty-five delegates from the United States, and the highlight of the meeting came when one of them, Professor Sidney Peck of the National Peace Action Council, called for mass action in the form of demonstrations at United States Embassies all over the world demanding the withdrawal of all US forces from South-East Asia.

A particularly significantly timed conference was held in February 1972 in Versailles. It is now known that at the time of this conference, The World Assembly for Peace and Independence of the People of Indochina, North Vietnamese forces had already been moving into position for the invasion of the South for over a month; 1,200 delegates from over eighty different countries attended this meeting which was sponsored by the World Peace Council. The major decision of the conference was to launch a series of massive demonstrations in the United States and other Western countries during the following April.

The North Vietnamese Government and the NLF High Command have never made any secret of the importance of the American anti-war movement to their cause. As early as 1966, for instance, a North Vietnamese paper described the American anti-war movement as 'a sharp knife stabbing them [the American force] in the back'. Radio Hanoi later said that it viewed 'the American People's protest movement' as a real second front against American Imperialism on the very soil of America itself.

Over the years a whole succession of messages have been sent from Hanoi to leaders of the American anti-war movement thanking them for their 'valiant struggle' against the 'aggressive designs' of their rulers. But, more importantly, news of demonstrations in the United States are broadcast to Viet Cong units in the field to give the impression that the enemy's home front is cracking and so fire them to make further efforts towards victory. A typical broadcast of this type was one of 13 November 1969 in which came the following words:

> 'A struggle which took to violence on 15 October 1969 will break out even more fiercely on 15 November. It will be coordinated by the New Mobilization Committee to End the Vietnam war, one of the largest anti-war organizations in the United States. This struggle will have more violence and be on a much larger and more elaborate scale in all US cities and state capitals. The seething struggle of US youths, students and people is urging us to arise and win final victory for the fatherland.'[6]

With the ending of American armed intervention there are already signs that plans are being made to transfer the whole weight of the campaign on to attacks on the government of South Vietnam itself.

6 'From Hanoi—With Thanks', *Reader's Digest*, February 1970, pp. 51–5

CHAPTER VIII

The Politics of Bloodshed: Conclusions

> 'War cannot for a single moment be
> separated from politics, politics
> are bloodless war, war is the
> politics of bloodshed.'
>
> MAO TSE-TUNG

At 4.30 a.m. on the morning of 12 September 1972 the police guards ending an uneventful night of patrolling round the perimeter of the Olympic Village outside Munich observed eight figures in two groups of four, dressed in athletes' track suits, climbing the high boundary fence. Thinking that the figures obviously represented nothing more sinister than athletes returning from an extra-early morning practice run, or possibly from a late night out, the guards resumed their peaceful patrol. Once inside the wire, however, the eight members of the Palestinian terrorist group Black September, for such they were, made straight for their target; the living quarters of the Israeli Olympic team located on the ground floor of a building less than 100 yards away. Two short bursts of automatic fire which ended the life of the Israeli team's top security man heralded the start of a day at the end of which fifteen people were to lie dead, and which was to give new and ominous meaning to the term 'propaganda of the deed'.

As the day bore on and one terrorist deadline for the commencement of the execution of their hostages succeeded another, and the crowds of detached onlookers with their transistors and ice cream lolling in the sun peered distantly at block 31, where the macabre drama that was to end in bloody shambles at Fuerstenfeldbruck air field that night was played out, ripples of alarm began to spread round the western world at the vulnerability of its much-vaunted 'open society' to the use of such desperate tactics by ruthless men prepared to take innocent life on the excuse that 'why should the whole world be having fun and entertainment while we suffer with all ears deaf to us?'[1]

'This time we shall force them to know that we are serious,' boasted the Black September men who carried out the Olympic Village attack, yet the episode was far from being Black September's first excursion into the 'politics of bloodshed'. The origins of the group go back to the destruction of Palestinian guerrilla power in Jordan by King Hussein's army in September 1970. It was formed in an atmosphere of vengeful bitterness by a number of members of Al Fatah, a bitterness directed not only against Israel but also against those Arab rulers such as Hussein who in the eyes of the guerrillas had 'betrayed' the Palestinian cause. Its first leader was an Al Fatah area commander named Ali Iyad, a powerful figure who because of his bald head and one eye was fond of calling himself 'the Arab answer to Moshe Dayan'. After his death in a gunfight with the Jordanian Army his sister became active in enrolling recruits in the new group.

Much of its recruiting was done in the bars and cafés of Beirut, a special effort being made to recruit not only young men and women who were likely to be adept at handling weapons, but also those who were good linguists, and had a flair for clandestine work or technical skills. Before long Black September also began to pick up recruits from some of the more Marxist—and revolutionary—minded members of Al Fatah, an organization with which it is reputed to retain contact through an official liaison link in the guise of an Al Fatah officer who has received training in Peking.

There is also evidence that Black September receives considerable support from and maintains links with Al Fatah through

[1] Statement left by Black September attack team and broadcast by Voice of Palestine radio station from Libya.

another organization known as Jihaz al-Rasd ('operation Network'), or more often 'Rasd', which some authorities consider actually controls Black September. Rasd was formed early in the 1960s with the original purpose of operating as an intelligence organization against Israel and carrying out security checks on Al Fatah recruits. The training of its first members was carried out by the Egyptian Intelligence Service. Before long its operations were extending far beyond their original scope. One of its main roles has been to become a primary source of fund-raising for Al Fatah, a duty which it performs through a variety of means, of which smuggling, including the smuggling of drugs into Europe from the Lebanon, is one.

Rasd also raises money for the cause through a number of legitimate business ventures, such as the Diplomatic Club in Rome which it controlled until its closure early in 1972. One of the frequenters of this club was a German businessman and his girlfriend, formerly one of Goebbels' favourite actresses. It would seem that this couple were engaged in gun-running since arms, including a machine gun, were found when their flat was raided after the Lydda airport massacre. Rasd's financial operations include the investing of money in European stocks, any profits made from its ventures being transferred to special bank accounts in Switzerland, Italy and West Germany.

Money is also brought in by obtaining contracts for carrying out acts of terrorism, including kidnapping, on behalf of other organizations, and on occasions even governments. One instance is related, of a North African government contracting with Rasd for the kidnapping of an exile living in Italy. On this occasion, however, the proposed victim offered his would-be kidnappers double the sum of money they had been promised if they would let him escape: an offer which Rasd promptly accepted, explaining to its hirers that the 'victim' could not be found. Rasd's leaders have a reputation for liking high living and its present leader Abu Hassan is well known for his tailor-made suits, Italian silk shirts, and love of expensive jewellery. His chief assistant is a German-educated engineer, Ghazi Husayni, who comes from the same family as that of the last Grand Mufti of Jerusalem.

Rasd is known to have established a considerable network of agents and cells in Europe. Amongst the recruits to these have been some European leftists and revolutionaries, including a number of women. Members of this network receive training in a Syrian base and are supplied with arms and explosives by Rasd. One major operation carried out by Rasd was the explosion at the Gulf Oil Refinery in Rotterdam in early 1971, which did a million dollars' worth of damage. This operation was carried out 'on contract' for a North African country by a unit of Rasd's European network, which included two French women. One of its main bases in Europe is reportedly in Lyons where there is a large Algerian community. There is also some reason to think that Rasd has established links with the Baendlistrasse Group in Zurich, which has been established as a coordinating centre for revolutionary activities. Its ramifications are said to include connections with clandestine meeting places and centres in Europe and the Far and Middle East. Nine of its members were arrested in Switzerland in 1972 on charges ranging from car stealing, burglary, and drug offences, to arson, arms smuggling, and attempted murder.

Black September operates in four- or five-man cells, only one of whose members (specially picked for liaison duties) is in touch with any other cell. The organization pays particular attention to maintaining good security, and any failings in this respect are considered to be the downfall of some other Palestinian guerrilla movements. It is said to be divided into four main commands responsible for operations in the Middle East, Africa, North and South America, and Europe respectively. Its members receive training in Al Fatah camps in Egypt, in Libya, and at its own special training base in Syria, where according to Israeli sources the facilities include those for training frogmen. Its links with Libya are particularly strong, and its leaders enjoy particularly good relations with the Libyan Army Chief of Staff, and a Libyan Army liaison officer is attached to the organization in a permanent capacity. Some recruits to the movement have also received training in Algeria where, as in Libya, they have received instruction from experts who have themselves been on special courses in Communist China or the Soviet Bloc.

Black September's first major operation was the assassination of the Jordanian Prime Minister in Cairo in 1971, one member of the four-man murder team employed on this occasion being a prominent member of Rasd. The other activities carried out by the group between that date and the Olympic Games massacre included the attempted assassination of the Jordanian Ambassador to London, aircraft hijacking, sabotage operation against a Dutch natural gas company with Israeli connections, and the blowing up of oil storage tanks in Trieste, probably with the help of Italian ultra-leftists. German factories working on contracts for Israel were also the object of Black September sabotage attacks, as was an oil pipeline near Hamburg. Five Jordanians living in West Germany were shot dead on the same day by Black September agents early in 1972 on suspicion of spying on the group's activities. Some members were also reportedly sent to Iran to prepare for operations in accord with the group's plan to strike at 'reactionary' Middle Eastern régimes.

It appears likely that Black September received some assistance from West German revolutionaries in the planning and carrying out the Berem and Ikrit Operation[2] as the group named the attack on the Israeli Olympic team, as well as previous attacks in Germany. As previously mentioned, members of the Baader-Meinhof group received training in Palestinian guerrilla camps at the time of its formation. Early in 1972 West German security authorities informed their opposite numbers in Lebanon that Baader and several other members of his group were believed to be on their way to Beirut travelling on forged passports. Baader was subsequently thought to have been seen in Beirut and an agreement to have been made by him on behalf of his group with Black September, the terms of which remain unknown. Despite the heavy toll taken of leading members of the Baader-Meinhof group by West German police action in following months, and the arrest of Baader himself, ties between Black September and surviving cells of the German organization are understood to have remained unbroken.

The growing degree of cooperation between the more extreme of today's revolutionary movements and the ease with which their members can at present avail themselves of the most modern facilities to travel more or less freely around the world in the course of their clandestine work was dramatically and brutally

[2] Named after two Israeli-occupied Arab villages on the Israel-Lebanon border.

demonstrated by the preliminary moves to the Lydda airport massacre—an episode that was also deeply illustrative of the growing fanaticism of such extremists.

The cold-blooded shooting down of twenty-seven persons at Lydda Airport in the early summer of 1972 was carried out by gunmen of the Japanese revolutionary United Red Army (Rengo Sekigun) acting on behalf of the Popular Front for the Liberation of Palestine (PFLP).

The Japanese United Red Army was formed in 1971 from the amalgamation of two left-wing groups. Most of its members are drawn from middle- or upper-class families, and its ideology is based upon a mixture of Marxist theory mixed with Samurai traditions. It first came into prominence in the headlines of the world's press when members hijacked an airliner in the spring of 1970. Even before the Lydda massacre it had established a particularly notorious reputation for itself by the inhuman treatment meted out to members of one of its groups who were accused of breaches of discipline. The group in question armed with guns and bombs was on the run from the police in the foothills of the Japanese Alps in the winter of 1971/72.

Led by Tsuneio Mori, the 27-year-old son of a hotel owner, and Hiroko Nagatia, the daughter of a well-respected business man, the group began to practise a curious new 'thought process' known as sokatsu. A young member was later to say, 'Once the process of sokatsu starts only death awaits you'.

The chief result of the practice of sokatsu seems to have been the granting of the right to Tsuneio Mori to order the trial and execution of any person who in any way caused him and the group displeasure. The 'offences' by members of the group which were dealt with in this way included the driving of a stolen car into a ditch and the wearing of ear-rings by a girl, this being considered 'bourgeois'.

One girl who hindered the group's freedom of movement by marrying and becoming pregnant was tortured: tied to a tree and left to freeze to death. Another girl was bound and gagged, and left to slowly suffocate in a cavity under the floor of a hut for three days and nights. One man was 'executed' by the two youngest members of the gang, his 19-year-old brothers, who stabbed him to death. Altogether fourteen people were put to death in ritualistic fashion and with varying degrees of barbarity in the space of two months.

Contact between the Popular Front for the Liberation of Palestine and the Japanese Red Army was probably first made in 1970 when the leader of the Palestinian movement Dr George Habash visited the Far East to address a revolutionary symposium in North Korea at which he made a speech, which included the following words:

'In the age of the revolution of peoples oppressed by the world imperialist system there can be no political or geographical boundaries or moral limits to the operations of the people's camp . . . in today's world no one is innocent, no one is neutral'.[3]

In the autumn of 1971 a film jointly produced by the Red Army and the PFLP made its appearance. Entitled *Declaration of World War by the Red Army and the PFLP*, it was shown in schools and universities all over Japan. About the same time a Red Army contact man took up residence in Beirut.

The only surviving member of the team of three Red Army gunmen which carried out the Lydda attack, Matsufuji Okamutu, said later that he was first brought into contact with the PFLP by a meeting with one of their commanders, known as Abu Ali, in Japan early in 1972. A fourth-year student of agriculture at the University of Kogoshma, Okamutu is the 24-year-old son of a retired schoolteacher, and one of his brothers is also a militant revolutionary and was involved in hijacking an airliner to North Korea in support of the Red Army's cause. Okamutu joined the Red Army in 1970. Selected as one of the Lydda attack team, he was told that when the time came his special role would be to act as bodyguard to the team's leader.

The mission commenced for Okamutu when he left Tokyo at the end of February 1972, flying by a Canadian Pacific flight to Montreal. Here he stayed at the Hilton Hotel until 4 March on which day he flew to Paris, where keeping up his high standard of accommodation he stayed for two days at the Grand Hotel before proceeding on the last leg of his journey, all of which was accomplished on a forged passport. Arriving in Beirut by air he met up with his three companions who had travelled

[3] *Newsweek*, 18 September 1972

separately by various routes, and the whole team journeyed together to a house in Baalbek from whence they were taken to PFLP training grounds for instruction in firing light automatic weapons and throwing grenades. They also learnt the most effective ways of employing incendiary bullets against airliners. At this time it was decided that all the team should commit suicide after the completion of their mission.

Training completed, Okamutu and his companions were flown back to Paris on an Air France plane on 23 May. From here they flew to Frankfurt, where they were provided with new forged passports. They next travelled by train to Rome where they stayed in a hotel and a pension until 30 May; on which day they received the weapons with which to carry out the attack, three Czech-made 7.62 automatic rifles, twelve magazines containing thirty rounds each, and some grenades. They then flew off to their assignment at Lydda.

After his capture following the shooting, in which all the members of the team besides himself died together with their victims, Okamutu said that he had never had any hatred for Israel. A spokesman of the PFLP, Bassam Zayid, explained to a correspondent that one of the main objects of the operation had been to 'raise the temperature' in the Middle East, and so provoke Israel into reprisals that would in turn rally Arab support for the guerrilla cause. He said that the Red Army gunmen had been given instructions not to open fire upon the passengers alighting from the French plane in which they travelled, but upon those in a plane landing ten minutes later, and upon the friends and relatives who had come to welcome them. The spokesman said:

> 'Our purpose was to kill as many people as possible at the airport. Israelis, of course, but anyone else who was there. There is a war going on in Palestine. People should know that . . .'[4]

He was also at pains to emphasize the cautionary effect the operation was hoped to have upon world opinion and would-be travellers, saying:

> 'This operation does effect the ordinary Englishman. He will be shocked. What horrible cold-blooded murderers. But he

4 *Guardian*, 1 June 1972

will think three times before coming to Israel. Why should I get killed, he will say to himself.'

As with Rasd and Black September the PFLP has its own network of agents and contacts in Europe and these are thought to have been of considerable assistance in easing the passage of the members of the Lydda murder team on their various journeyings and in providing them with material assistance. Their arms were probably delivered to them in Rome for instance by Italian ultra-leftists. Reports have spoken of members of the PFLP being in Dublin in the spring of 1972 for the purpose of a conference with members of the Provisional IRA.

Keeping a sharp eye upon this upsurge of activity and intermingling on the part of terrorist and revolutionary movements, and despite periodic and selective official Soviet outbursts against the use of terrorism by official Soviet spokesmen, stands the Soviet Union's political intelligence service, the KGB, together with its counterpart in the lesser countries of the Soviet bloc. From time to time their hand can be glimpsed seeking to exploit or divert this activity to serve their own ends.

There would seem no doubt that members of the Turkish People's Liberation Army, the revolutionary organization which was responsible for the kidnapping and murder of British technicians from the NATO radar station in Northern Turkey in 1971, were enabled to obtain training in Palestinian guerrilla camps through the good offices of Soviet agents based in Damascus; nor that arms were smuggled into Turkey for the use of the organization by members of the East German and Bulgarian intelligence services. There have been indications of attempts by Soviet agents to infiltrate revolutionary movements in both France and Belgium; and subsequent to the rupture in relations between the Soviet and Egyptian Governments there were reports of Soviet small arms being delivered direct to Al Fatah. Soviet efforts in the field of support to various liberation movements in arms in Africa, the Far East and Latin America have been detailed in the previous chapter.

One revolutionary coordinating centre, in which the KGB as well as Cuban agents are known to be particularly interested, is the Committee for International Affairs recently established in Chile. Inspired and largely led by Tupamaro elements its primary aim is the coordination of and the provision of aid to guerrilla movements in Uruguay, Argentina, Brazil, Bolivia, Chile, Peru and Ecuador. But its tentacles also stretch out to Algeria, North Korea, Communist China and Egypt.

While in all probability it will for some time continue to be the established revolutionary movements that are involved in major campaigns in the Third World, such exponents of 'propaganda of the deed' as Black September or guerrilla and terrorist foco groups such as the Baader-Meinhof group or the Angry Brigade, it should not be forgotten that the main threat to Western society probably comes from revolutionary organizations that are still in a preparatory stage of their activity. Although mindful of the probable or, in some cases, inevitable need for the use of violence on their part to achieve power when the time is ripe, for the time being they are concentrating largely upon propaganda and agitational activity to lead to the formation of well-trained, indoctrinated and organized 'revolutionary parties', along the lines advocated by Lenin, capable (or so they hope) of 'seizing the leadership of the people' at some moment of crisis; and concentrating also upon undermining the existing social and Governmental system by playing upon the fears and frustrations of every possible type.[5] Once again the latter part of their activity is along the lines favoured and so well outlined by Lenin, and is aimed at exposing the 'brutality', corruption, feebleness or inefficiency of present rulers and illustrating the fact that no progress along the road to 'the ideal state' can be hoped for without their total removal and the institution of a completely different 'system'.

An American author, Eugene H. Methvin, has described the revolutionary agitator, as the breed has now evolved, engaged upon these sort of undermining tactics, as both the orchestrator and conductor of all the discontent that exists in society, fanning each spark of friction into a searing flame, ever scanning society to locate and nurture new grievances and find ways of turning each mild complaint into a feeling of bitter hatred; then, when all is ready for the 'performance', calling into play each alienated

[5] Typical of such groups are the various bodies affiliated to the Brussels-based Trotskyist IV International in Western Europe and elsewhere, among which there are increasing signs of international cooperation.

section of society from the conductor's stand, finally producing a grand climax of discord and conflict. A climax from which the power bestowed upon him by his own tightly knit and disciplined organization will allow him to emerge as undisputed master.

The description is apt, and well fits both those revolutionary agitators who see their chances of seizing power as being through violence at some moment of national or international violence, but also those from orthodox Communist parties as nowadays seek to obtain power through the normal constitutional machinery in order to impose their brand of revolution from above, although it should never be forgotten that no Communist party, even in Western countries, has ever yet altogether renounced the possibility of using violence to achieve its ends if all else fails; and many parties in the Third World stand fast in the belief that the way to power can only in the long run lie through violence on the streets or the rural guerrilla campaign.

The basic difference in the attitude of mind between the modern democratic politician and the committed revolutionary can nowhere be more clearly seen than in their attitude to the use of violence. To the great majority of democratic politicians the use of violence is a very last resort, something to be avoided on either an internal or international scale at almost any cost; whereas, to the revolutionary, violence and non-violent agitation are merely two complementary weapons, to be used either as alternatives or in combination as circumstances demand.

This inter-relationship of non-violent and violent action is basic to modern revolutionary thought, and hence the relevance of the quotation at the head of this chapter. For it was above all of revolutionary warfare that Mao Tse-tung was speaking, and it is political and psychological objectives that the modern revolutionary has in mind rather than chances of outright military victory, when he speaks of embarking upon an 'armed struggle'.

Most revolutionaries of the recent past, Marxists and non-Marxists alike, have realized that the chances of obtaining outright military victory against the formidable forces ranged against them are slight or even non-existent. They see, however, their chances of success as lying mainly in their ability to undermine public confidence in the régime they seek to overthrow by subjecting it to a period of prolonged and violent pressure, during which its inability either to protect its friends or destroy the revolutionaries will be repeatedly demonstrated, the Government will be forced to introduce more and more repressive measures, and life for the ordinary citizen will become more and more unpleasant. Finally, it is hoped, a state of mind is introduced in the general public in which almost anything, including surrender to the revolutionaries' demands, seems preferable to the continuing chaos and bloodshed.

Some of the essential ingredients for inclusion in the recipe of armed action and psychological warfare and propaganda needed to bring about this state of affairs were described once by the Brazilian urban guerrilla leader Carlos Marighella shortly before which almost anything, including surrender to the revolutionaries' awareness that each armed attack or act of terrorism should itself be looked on as an act of propaganda, as each such incident was sure to be immediately reported by the mass news media. The news media and all other means of mass communication, and the oral spreading of rumours should be made intensive use of for the spreading of specially manufactured reports and rumours aimed at discrediting the Government. False plans of impending guerrilla action should also be allowed to fall into the hands of the authorities, and the time of the security services wasted in investigating false warnings.

Marighella also advocated that individual examples of Government mistakes and corruption should be eagerly exposed in a fashion which make them seem to be typical of a prevailing state of affairs; Government counter action such as censorship should become a particular target for attack. At the same time the guerrillas should build public support by persistently intervening and making their presence felt in all questions relating to the life of the people. They should also appear as their champions by fomenting and supporting strikes and interruptions of work in universities. He stated that even though such stoppages by workers and students lasted only a short time they could cause a Government serious damage if they occurred 'endlessly', one after the other, in authentic guerrilla fashion, at different points in a given area.

In addition energetic measures must be taken to ensure through intimidation or appeal that those members of the public who were unwilling to support the revolutionary movement did not at least

13—S • •

do anything against it. A sustained campaign to undermine the country's economy and damage the interests of the business community should also be launched, and efforts made to disrupt the tax collection system.

Such a combination of armed action and terrorism, political subversion and propaganda as advised thus by such a leading Latin American revolutionary (and which in many features shows a remarkable similarity to the campaign waged in practice by the Provisional IRA) is not aimed solely at impressing the inhabitants of the particular country in which the revolution is taking place with the government's inability to cope with the situation, nor at demoralizing the forces actively opposing the revolutionaries, but equally importantly at creating the impression abroad that the régime concerned is not only oppressive and corrupt, but tottering on the edge of collapse, and that the revolutionaries' inevitable success is merely a matter of time. The object of this is to persuade foreign governments, which are or might be inclined to becoming involved in giving financial or material aid to the régime under threat, that the régime's cause is hopeless and further efforts to save it fruitless, and to force foreign business concerns, which may be an important stabilizing economic influence in the country, to acknowledge that the time has come to cut their losses and get out or possibly attempt to come to some 'arrangement' with the revolutionaries.

The international effect of internal revolution cannot infrequently be decisive on the outcome of the revolutionary campaign itself; an American observer of the Cuban revolution, Robert Tabor, has written of the course events took in that country:

'The Fidelistas [Castroite Forces] succeeded in Cuba, not because Fidel was a master of guerrilla tactics—he was not—but because he understood what it was he had to do. His purpose, as we discussed it when we first met, at the very beginning of his campaign, was to create in the capital the climate of collapse.

'This meant, first of all, making it clear to the outside world that an active military force existed and was beyond the control of the Batista military.

'It meant, secondly, impairing the Cuban economy, and spreading disorder in the Cuban business community, so that foreign investors would begin to ask themselves whether there was not some better alternative to Batista.

'As banking and business credits became less available, and the bad publicity for the Batista régime mounted, the supporters of the régime, business men and high military officers, began to look about for alternatives, or began to plan their exit . . .

'When the régime—as in the Cuban case—can no longer preserve the stability of the economy (in other words when foreign investment is threatened) it must fail, simply because it will no longer be in the interests of anyone who supports it.'[6]

The amount of thought and planning given by modern revolutionaries to obtaining international publicity by their deeds, in order to ensure that international pressure in favour of surrender to their demands is brought not only upon the Government they seek to overthrow, but also upon others friendly to it and upon whom it leans, is still not always properly realized, despite its often central position to the revolutionaries' strategy. It has loomed particularly large in colonial-type revolutionary situations. Two years before EOKA commenced operations in Cyprus, for instance, Grivas was writing in Greece that the essential factor in launching any successful revolt on the island would be the arousing of:

'. . . international public opinion, especially among the allies of Greece, by deeds of heroism and self-sacrifice which will focus attention on Cyprus until our aims are achieved. The British must be continuously harried and beset until they are obliged by international diplomacy, exercised through the United Nations, to examine the Cyprus problem and settle it in accordance with the desire of the Cypriot people.'[7]

The manipulation of international opinion in order to exert pressure on the Government of the United States and other nations to desist from giving aid to the government of South Vietnam, as has been mentioned in this study, has always been a

[6] Robert Tabor, *The Techniques of the Guerrilla Fighter*, *Revolution*, Vol. 1, No. 6 (1963), pp. 96–109
[7] Grivas, *The Memoirs of General Grivas*, Longman, Green (London, 1964), p. 204

major factor in the minds of the Viet Cong and North Vietnamese High Commands, and, as we have also seen, the IRA needs no lessons in the power of international propaganda. Despite the immense resources available to it the American government has only managed a remarkably inadequate response to the storm of propaganda unleashed against it over the involvement of its armed forces in Vietnam; as a consequence its just case has to a large degree gone by default. In the same way until very recently there was little or no sign that the British Government was making any adequate attempt to reply to the world-wide propaganda campaign of the IRA, despite the obvious opportunities for exposure provided by the barbaric nature of that movement's activities.

A feature of revolutionary propaganda both on the national and international level has been the deliberate instigation of a belief in the infallibility of modern guerrilla and revolutionary techniques. It is a theory hardly borne out by the facts. The list of failures by instigators of revolutionary warfare in the post-war world is nearly as long as that of their successes. Guerrilla forces engaged in revolutionary campaigns of varying types have, for instance, been crushingly defeated in Malaya, fought at least to a standstill in Vietnam, and despite substantial external aid so far have been remarkably unsuccessful both in Southern Africa and, with the exception of the Tupamaros, in Latin America. Where they have been successful they have owed their victory almost always not to military or technical brilliance but to adroit exploitation of the weakness of irresolute governments and the desire of the rulers and population of tired colonial powers for 'peace at any price'. Yet despite these facts the legend of the invincibility of revolutionary forces and techniques of subversion continues to be used with effect to bring fear and defeatism into the minds and hearts of those who may be their next chosen target.

Side by side with this approach have gone consistent attempts to glamorize the use of violence when used for revolutionary or 'progressive' purposes. Not only is the impression being created, particularly among susceptible groups of young people, that 'anything goes', but a deliberate attempt is being made to create the belief that progress can only come through violence

190

and that 'the system' is so sick that all attempts to bring about change through reform and evolution are mere time-wasting efforts doomed to failure. The focus of the revolutionary, once in large degree centred upon university students, is now being spread to encompass children of a very low age. In the Western world such propaganda is spread through a number of special 'pupil power' and other school movements which seek to indoctrinate children with a thoroughgoing hatred, not only of present educational systems but of all established authority. In the Third World brief indoctrination of very young children is to a growing extent quite frequently followed by their enrolment in the ranks of a terrorist or guerrilla movement and training in the use of arms.

A recent example of exploitation of the very young by revolutionaries has been provided by the activities of the Popular Front for the Liberation of the Occupied Arab Gulf (PFLOAG), a movement which is basically Maoist in outlook and whose main links are with Communist China, although its leaders also have some contact with Moscow. The movement, which is estimated to consist of 600-800 hard-core guerrillas, has for some time been carrying on an armed campaign in the Dhofar province of Oman. Recent reports have stated that the movement has been recruiting boys as young as six or seven, who are taken from their homes and sent to be indoctrinated with Maoist thought at the 'Lenin School' in South Yemen. Many boys under twelve are said to have been trained in the use of recoilless rifles, rocket launchers, and heavy machine guns. Most of these are intended to return to Dhofar to swell the ranks of the PFLOAG guerrillas, but others are intended for despatch to other Gulf states such as Abu Dhabi, Qatar, or Dubai, where they will be expected to wait for the call to action.

The events of almost every month, if not sometimes almost every week, of the latter part of 1972 seemed to clearly show that the days when the threat of terrorism and armed action by revolutionaries could be considered a matter purely confined to the Third World were certainly over, and that a wide range of countries across the world now to a greater or lesser degree faced threats to their internal security more serious than any they had known for many years. Included in these countries were most of the leading Western democracies, in which a debate of growing intensity began on how best to meet this new peril.[8]

This debate has ranged on the one hand from proposals for the introduction of draconian measures which in fact would be entirely contrary to the traditions of the countries concerned, repugnant to their populations, and which no conceivable government would ever be likely to implement; to suggestions on the other hand that all that really needs to be done is to speed up social reform, remove all possible causes of injustice and all will be well. Also to be heard were defeatist views on the impossibility of building effective defences against tactics of terrorism and subversion within a democratic framework.

The problems of maintaining internal security within a democracy without infringing basic freedoms have never been simple. For many years before the last decade most Western democratic governments had relied heavily on the belief that their populations had reached a stage of development wherein they were prepared to play their political 'games' according to strict rules and within limits which ruled out the use of serious violence. That this is no longer fully justified is now all too apparent, and consequently the services charged with safeguarding life, limb, and property within its boundaries face a task of new dimensions, a task already complicated enough by the appearance of the 'open society' and the 'permissive age'.

The extent to which security forces in democracies have the odds loaded against them in attempting preventive action, even when the chances of a terrorist attack or another outrage are clear under prevailing conditions, can be glimpsed from details of the background of the Olympic Games massacre. Although a manual prepared by the Bavarian police authorities months before the Games for the guidance of its officers clearly mentioned the possibility of extremist elements seizing the opportunity the games afforded to commit some violent demonstration upon the 'public stage', their problems in preventing any such incidents were almost insuperable. There were a total of 390 radical left-wing groups in West Germany at the time, of which a large

8 The story of the Angry Brigade, small-scale and amateurish though the operations of this group were, show clearly that Britain cannot be considered proof against prevailing dangers.

percentage were listed as subversive or potentially subversive. Altogether there were 219 political organizations for foreign nationals in the country with a total of 1,021 branches, and of these organizations ten were for Palestinian Arabs and had between them 142 local branches. In addition the police estimated that there were some 800 'strong points' or bases for ultra-left activity spread throughout the nation.

In a country deluged by foreign students and workers the number of Arab residents or visitors alone amounted to at least 36,000, of whom some 3,000 were Palestinian students.

On a local level the Olympic Village at Munich needed 5,000 workers to run it, many of whom came from outside the area and a considerable proportion from outside the country: a survey, for instance, showed that the kitchen staff of just under 1,000 comprised eighty-seven different nationalities. To top all this the security regulations in force at the Olympic Village had to be eased shortly after the Games commenced in the face of repeated protests from some of the mass of journalists present, that their movements were being needlessly restricted.

The conditions described above are certainly not purely confined to Germany and could in fact be said to be fairly typical of those now coming to prevail in most Western countries. But although such conditions obviously make defence against terrorist or revolutionary tactics vastly more difficult, they are far from making them impossible, given proper governmental consideration and determination and the proper cooperation of all law-abiding forces and nations. The key in the first place is certainly international cooperation amongst all like-minded nations who recognize the dangers of the present situation. In particular, there is an obvious need for the closer cooperation of the police and security forces, and for this reason the setting-up of a special office in Scotland Yard to coordinate international police investigations into the various outbreaks of terrorism that occurred in the autumn of 1972 is much to be welcomed.

Interpol would seem likely to prove a somewhat unsuitable instrument for such liaison, even if changes are made in the article of its code which at present debars it from dealing with politically motivated offences (except for aircraft hijacking, and even this is a recent exception).

The aim of all such international cooperation should in the first place be to make the movement of members of terrorist organizations, professional revolutionaries, and other like subversives about the world a very much more difficult business than it is at present. Such elements openly regard themselves as being at war with society, and there is no need for society therefore to regard their 'right' of free movement to be more important than its own survival. A second aim should be to smash the growing terrorist/revolutionary infrastructure which is making possible the growing cooperation of such movements in different countries. An infrastructure which has been described by a young Palestinian in the following words:

'... We have our own businesses like the Diplomat Club in Rome, which the authorities closed down last April. But there are a lot more. There are travel agencies that can arrange things. There are laundries and grocery stores. But of course these businesses are not solely businesses. They are also collection agencies, mail drops, meeting places, points of contact.'[9]

The recent decision of the United States Government to require all visitors, and even those in transit, to have visas before being allowed to enter the country has much to recommend it and could well be considered by other nations anxious to cut down the current level of politically inspired violence. Its justification lies in the fact that official investigations have revealed that during 1971–2 some 5,000 persons entered the United States on the claim of being in transit, only to quickly disappear. Upon their eventual 'surfacing' many were found to have come into possession of complete sets of forged papers and the evidence was that some were involved in the planning of acts of terrorism against a wide range of targets.

The present difficulties facing British security men in dealing with the problem of the entry of members of extremist organizations into the country were illustrated in an article in the *Evening Standard* of 9 October 1972 discussing the movements of members of Arab terrorists. It stated:

'Over the weekend at least eight such men have been reported to have arrived here and disappeared. The police

[9] *Time*, 25 April 1972

face an almost impossible job—for the men may arrive with an Arab passport and then stay or leave with another, not necessarily an Arab passport.'

The full scale of this problem can perhaps be seen from the fact that London Airport alone handles some 900 aircraft a day and deals with about 2 million passengers each month.

Another encouraging development which would seem to indicate determination on the part of the American Government to come to grips with current problems has been the appointment of a Cabinet-level committee, which includes such high-level members of Nixon's Government as the Defense Secretary, Melvin Laird, Henry Kissinger, and the Directors of the CIA and FBI, to take charge of a 'war against terrorism'. It would seem that the establishment of similar types of committees might well be an advantage in other Western countries including Britain.

Some form of permanent body to speed the flow of information on terrorist/subversive techniques and tactics between Western European nations (along with friendly nations outside Europe), and to plan and coordinate counter action, will almost certainly be a necessity of the future. Possibly such a body could either be brought under the auspices of the European community or within the command establishment of NATO on the lines of the office already functioning for the study of subversion and counter-subversion within the headquarters of the South-East Asia Treaty Organization.

It is profoundly to be hoped that the Hague convention on measures to prevent aircraft hijacking will prove a workable instrument, and that the various conferences and negotiations that have been taking place on the subject will prove fruitful. It is possible to feel much sympathy with the feeling of frustration of leaders of many airline pilots' associations at the repeated delays that have occurred in attempts to reach agreement on the pre-vention of hijacking and on the strengthening of airport security in the past. Another matter upon which there is urgent need for international agreement and action is finding ways of making explosives and detonators sold for commercial purposes more easily traceable as to their source of manufacture. The determina-tion of some members of the United Nations to protect the interests of guerrilla groups engaged in 'crusades' in Southern

Africa and some other areas has now almost completely ruled out the chances of agreement by that body on any practical measures to combat the spread of terrorism, and consequently the best hope for this would seem to lie in an urgent attempt at bilateral agreements between like-minded nations.

Many of the questions that will have to be answered by individual Western governments, in countries with long liberal traditions, are of more than usual difficulty. None, for instance, will want to reverse present policies and bar their doors to genuine refugees from persecution and oppression. On the other hand, if the fight against the spread of terrorism and allied techniques is to be truly effective it is permissible to wonder for how much longer it will be possible to take a relaxed attitude towards cities such as London being used as free havens by professional revolutionaries, where, in the words of one Scotland Yard officer, they can sit in selected rendezvous: 'eating jelly and cakes and brownbread and butter sandwiches blithely discussing availabilities of weapons and supplies of explosives.'[10] Free from any serious threat of interference with their planning.

The creation of a special highly mobile anti-terrorist unit by the West German Government may well start a trend which will spread to other Western countries where no such forces now exist. A howl of indignation from all the usual pro-revolutionary forces can be expected should this come to pass. But whilst a tight check on the use and operations of such forces must always be kept by the governments concerned, it does seem possible that their mere existence might act as a considerable deterrent to the repetition of any such episodes as that at Munich.

An essential ingredient in the containment of terrorism and revolutionary activity is the possession of adequate information services, through which a government can expose the plans and activities of those who seek to undermine it, defend itself and the security forces under its command against attacks by hostile propaganda, and explain to the people the need for the various security measures it may be necessary to adopt. The rare existence of such services would seem to be a weak point in the internal defences of most Western countries at the present time. In Britain it would not appear that Government information

10 *Newsweek*, 18 September 1972

services are even remotely attuned to the sort of duties they would have to perform in any sudden internal emergency. The counter-insurgency expert Brigadier Kitson, writing in his book *Low Intensity Operations* on the closely related topic of psychological warfare, has pointed to the serious shortcomings in the facilities available to the British Army in this field, compared with those of a number of other European forces.

British politicians are fond of maintaining that the answer to internal unrest and subversion does not lie in 'repression'. But neither can it safely be said to lie solely or even mainly along the path of reform. Those who believe this underrate the fanaticism and the skill and adaptability of the modern revolutionary. The answer can only lie in the combination of a programme of social advance with the introduction of measures which, while not 'repressive' in the sense of being brutal or harsh, give adequate pause for reflection to those slowly but steadily growing numbers who believe that the shortest and most effective road to power lies not through the ballot box, but through the bomb and bullet. In this combination lies the best hope of arresting the present wave of political violence, which now so clearly threatens the foundations of Western society.

Index